What Your Doctor & Your Pastor

Want You to

Know about

Depression

What Your Doctor & Your Pastor

Want You to

Know about

Depression

R. Lanny Hunter, M.D.
Victor L. Hunter, M.Div., D.Min.

CHALICE®
P R E S S
ST. LOUIS, MISSOURI

Biblical quotations, unless otherwise noted, are from the *New Revised Standard Version Bible*, copyright 1989, Division of Christian Education of the National Council of the Churches of Christ in the United States of America. Used by permission. All rights reserved.

Cover art: Getty Images
Cover and interior design: Elizabeth Wright

This book is printed on acid-free, recycled paper.

Visit Chalice Press on the World Wide Web at
www.chalicepress.com

10 9 8 7 6 5 4 3 2 1   04 05 06 07 08 09

Library of Congress Cataloging–in–Publication Data

Hunter, R. Lanny.
  What your doctor and your pastor want you to know about depression /
R. Lanny Hunter, M.D. and Victor L. Hunter.
      p. cm.
  ISBN 0-8272-4248-4 (pbk. : alk. paper)
  1. Depression, Mental–Popular works. 2. Depression,
Mental–Religious aspects–Christianity. I. Hunter, Victor L. II.
Title.
  RC537.H866 2004
  362.2'5–dc220
                                                    2003026537

Printed in the United States of America

Contents

A Word to the Reader   1

1 On Being a Whole Person*   3

2 The Physical Disease   17

3 Treating the Physical Disease   39

4 The Social Disease   53

5 The Psychological Disease   63

6 The Spiritual Dis-ease   79

7 The Terminal Disease   97

Postscript: A Cloud of Witnesses   113

Prayer for those Unable to Dance   115

*Each chapter begins with a selection from "The Man Who Couldn't Dance," a fictional story told in seven parts.

For those who suffer from depression,
and those who live with them.

A Word to the Reader

Our desire in this book is to address you personally as companions in the difficult, painful, and deeply human journey through depression. We have written it from the perspectives of our two disciplines (medicine and theology) and our two professions (physician and pastor), drawing on extensive reading, reflection, and our years of clinical and pastoral experience.

Among the sources providing information, particularly statistics, for this book are the following:

Akron Law Review (Fall 1987)

American Foundation for Suicide Prevention

"Anxiety and Your Brain," *Newsweek* (February 24, 2003)

Capps, Donald, *Men, Religion, and Melancholia* (New Haven, Conn.:Yale University Press, 1997)

Centers for Disease Control and Prevention

"How Your Mind Can Heal Your Body," *Time* 161, no. 3 (January 20, 2003)

Jamison, K.R., *Night Falls Fast* (New York: Knopf, 1999)

Jamison, K.R., *Touched With Fire* (New York: Free Press, 1993)

McIntosh, J.L., "1998 Official Final Statistics: U.S.A. Suicide"

Missouri Law Review (Winter 1992)

National Alliance for the Mentally Ill

National Institute of Mental Health

National Mental Health Association

National Vital Statistics Reports

U. S. Public Health Service Reports, Washington, D.C., 1999

Whittier Law Review (1991)

We also want you to know that we have both experienced clinical depression and are survivors of it. You are not alone.

R. Lanny Hunter, M.D.
Victor L. Hunter, M.Div., D.Min.

1

Each chapter of this book begins with a selection from "The Man Who Couldn't Dance," a fictional story of an individual's experience of depression. The story's seven parts introduce the chapters of this book and illustrate their concepts.

The Man Who Couldn't Dance: PART ONE

Ernest ignored the sign reserving the lane for carpoolers and cut his Audi sharply into the line of traffic, cutting off the car behind him. The driver leaned on his horn, and Ernest blared back. He was late for the archdiocesan board meeting. Maybe the car pool lane violation would get him five minutes. Was a traffic violation a venial or mortal sin? Who cared? He felt the weight of The Fall. A fallen man in a fallen world, he believed in original sin. There was something reasonable, if not reassuring, about the curse of original sin. He wished some of his sins *were* original. Life had become so banal, his existence so barren, that he was cursed with *un*original sin.

Ernest had had trouble getting out of bed that morning after another insomniac night. He asked himself, "Why?" His days passed so grimly that he welcomed anger as a fillip to the slough of depression. He got up every morning ready to pick a fight. Willing to take on all comers. Indiscriminate verbal assaults. He hated it. Hated himself. But he couldn't stop. "Why?" At night, staring at the ceiling, he imagined himself creeping through the labyrinth of his mind, guttering torch of consciousness held aloft to light his way, like Diogenes going about the world seeking an honest man, except he searched the recesses of his mind asking, "Why?" He explored the tortuous pathways searching for meaning, descending down, down, to the dismal, dank subterranean grotto where the pit viper lay coiled. Primordial memories fused with primitive emotions. Malevolence and melancholy seeped like steam through the fissures of his existence. His Giorgio Armani became jungle fatigues, and he once again walked point through a festering shadowland waiting for the bullet, the bayonet, the booby trap. Would it be blindness, bowels hanging out, balls blown away, or sitting in a wheelchair the rest of his life doing his business in a piss-bag? He knew there were worse things than dying, but his compass wouldn't register true north. He climbed back up to the bunker of his brain, crept out, and sat on a berm. Studied the concertina wire that encircled his position. Was he captive or secure? Dawn finally came.

Daylight streamed through the clerestory windows of Ernest's bedroom. Light, but no enlightenment. Mary stirred beside him. He closed his eyes, feigning sleep. She slipped quietly out of bed, wary of provoking a mood. An hour later, she returned, dressed for work. "Ernie," she said softly, "remember, you have a meeting this morning." He nodded without opening his eyes. A conversation was more than he could bear. He heard Mary's car leave the driveway and tried to summon the energy to crawl out of bed. It wasn't the lack of sleep. It was the stone-bone weariness. There was a hole in his chest where his Heart had been. A hole in his mind where his Being had been. A hole in heaven where his God had been. Ernest had no reserves of energy, but with an act of will, he heaved himself out of bed and went to the shower. He stood under the hot water a long time, letting the stream pummel him. He glanced at his waterproof watch—government issue, just like jungle boots, right and left, one each—a relic of his tour of duty. He was cutting his meeting close.

Ernest accelerated across three lanes of traffic to the exit ramp. The skyline glinted in the morning sun. He could see the corporate high-rise that housed his office. Two blocks beyond it was Saint Thomas, a parish church whose name was a prescient corollary for this stage of his religious existence. The inner-city church squatted on five invaluable acres amidst the skyscrapers, but it didn't have enough money to finance its gospel or good works. The first traffic light was gridlocked. He would be late, after all. Tough. Life was a series of belated arrivals now. Crossroads, crossed up, and crossed out. Ernest wheeled the Audi into the church parking lot. The diocese hoped his financial skills could resurrect the good works. He hoped the diocesan gospel could resurrect his diminished life. Again, Ernest asked himself, "Why?" Down the long decades to these constricted days, *push* had finally come to *shove* him, and for the life of him, Ernest didn't know "why." There was no "why." Or "what" or "how." Perhaps a "when." A dreadful, dark, final "when"...

CHAPTER ONE

On Being a Whole Person

Vanity of vanities, says the Teacher,
vanity of vanities! All is vanity.
What do people gain from all the toil
at which they toil under the sun?...

I said to myself, "Come now, I will make a test of pleasure; enjoy
yourself." But again, this also was vanity...

I searched with my mind how to cheer my body...

Then I considered all that my hands had done and the toil I had
spent in doing it, and again, all was vanity and a chasing after
wind, and there was nothing to be gained under the sun.

ECCLESIASTES 1:2–3; 2:1, 3, 11

Ernest wasn't just angry. He was unstable. He wasn't sad. He was sick. He wasn't down. He was depressed. Depression is a disease that afflicts one in five Americans. It affects all races and all ages, both men and women, the rich and the poor, the powerful and the powerless, the hero and the coward, those of high moral character and the corrupt, people of every religion and those who profess no faith at all. The disease may be mild and silently steal a life. It may be severe and immobilizing. It can be a terminal illness.

Depression is a tough enemy that gives no quarter. It skins you alive. It sucks the vitality out of life. Days are dark and nights are long. Clouds don't have a silver lining. Hank Williams once thrilled the Grand Ole Opry crowd with his lyrics, "Then Jesus came like a stranger in the night. Praise the Lord, I saw the light!" He strummed the last chord and walked backstage to wild applause as Minnie Pearl waited in the wings. The story goes that Hank said, "that's the trouble, Minnie. There ain't no light." Not only does depression destroy the life of the person who has the disease, it touches everyone—spouses, children, friends, employers, coworkers, and associates. It wounds even chance creatures—critter, human, or inanimate object—unlucky enough to cross the path of depressed persons when they are in one of their moods. The depressed suffer and they inflict suffering. This poses complex questions for everyone circling in the orbit of depression. It poses especially complex problems for religious people because depression seeps into God.

Medicine and Theology

This book is written from both a medical and a theological perspective, and it draws on the Christian tradition and our own experience of faith. As part of this tradition, we will begin each chapter with a passage of scripture and end each chapter with a prayer from the broad history of the church. This will serve as a reminder that depression is not a stranger to the life of faith. Furthermore, we make no apology for our Christian perspective. Henry S. Levinson, addressing Harvard Divinity School, spoke eloquently of the role religion has played in the human story. Quoting Lionel Trilling, Levinson said, "If we are in a balloon over an abyss, let us at least value the balloon. If night is all around us, then what light we have is precious. If there is no life to be seen in the great emptiness, our companions are to be cherished, as are we ourselves." Levinson himself continues, "Religions were among the central institutions to gather precious light, to provide forms of cherished companionship, to present disciplines for individuals in their solitude—meditative, morally, interrogatory, prayerful, humorous." Levinson ends by summarizing George Santayana's message: The truly religious ... "love what good life there is...[l]ove what chances there are for more good life, both in solitude and in society...[h]ope for and work for and enjoy large life, more large life—that is, more life worth living. And our sense of what makes life large, what makes it worth living, is very much derived from our religious traditions in their diversity, if and when we're lucky enough to have them."[1]

Just as we need vocational, recreational, social, and artistic dimensions in order to be whole persons, we must have a spiritual dimension to life to be whole persons. Philosophical underpinnings are essential to the considered life. Persons who never bring their adult, critical faculties to bear on the subject of humankind's origin,

---

[1]Henry S. Levinson, "The William James Lecture for 2000–01," *Harvard Divinity Bulletin,* vol. 30, no. 2 (Summer/Fall 2001): 5.

place, purpose, and potential destiny shirk their responsibility as perceptive, thinking human beings. Cosmic questions, if not answered, must at least be asked.

Every person, in fact, does have a spiritual/philosophical/creedal dimension to his or her life because everyone lives by some myth. To choose a myth is to operate by faith, and any system of faith by which one attempts to construct a worldview is a religion. Religions don't have to use God-talk. Rationalism, atheism, Marxism, naturalism, and scientism are philosophies that can be, and often are, embraced with a narrowly focused ideological fanaticism. The flaw of scientism lies in believing that the scientific method can investigate all forms of human experience, and that given time and resources, science can quantify every life riddle in weight, mass, and chemical reaction. It's a futile hope, as it ignores the realm of the heart and the spirit. In fact, pure science ventures into the realm of faith. When natural scientists project their discipline to its boundaries, they have moved beyond science to metaphysics—to myth and faith. When scientists attempt to prove their myths by experiential confirmation (existentialism)— not scientific methodology—they have not entered the arena of proof. They have joined theologians in the domain of *story*. On the other hand, theologians—seduced by the absolutist claims of scientism—have forsaken their vocations of reflection, intuition, and inspiration in the mistaken notion that their discipline, if furthered by the scientific method, would be accorded more credibility. They, too, have lost their way. A myth—even a true myth—can't be proven using the scientific method. When both scientist and theologian pursue their vocations with integrity, they recognize the limits of their disciplines and treat knowledge with humility.

As a medical doctor and a pastor, we will combine our two disciplines—medicine and theology—to explore depression's causes and symptoms and its connection to the physical, emotional, behavioral, social, and spiritual dimensions of life. In addition to education and insight, we hope to give practical suggestions, support, and encouragement to depressed persons and their families, friends, and associates. There are only two things you can do about depression. First, acknowledge it. Second, get help! The grim beast is a formidable adversary. There are no easy answers and no quick fixes, but there is help and there is hope.

The Fallacy of Dualism

One strength of Eastern mystical traditions is their belief that mind and body are indivisible. In Western culture, the tendency toward dualism confuses clear thinking about the nature of humanity. Dualism divides human nature into physical *or* spiritual, body *or* soul, biological *or* psychological, nature *or* nurture, secular *or* religious, personal *or* social. These are artificial distinctions and they thwart attempts to find answers to humanity's questions and problems. The dualistic world is fragmented and can't be whole.

In the early part of the twentieth century, discussions of mental illness often attempted to distinguish what was *organic* and what was *functional.* Organic illnesses were caused by physical abnormalities that could be studied under a microscope or through blood tests. These diseases were biologically based and were understood as *real* illnesses. Functional illnesses, on the other hand, did not arise from biology but in dysfunctional behavior when dealing with life's issues and stress. They were expressions of psychological factors, such as conflict between a person's emotions and intellect or when a person's unconscious memories of the past impact present experiences (Sigmund Freud's hypothesis). These diseases were psychologically based, and weren't real (biological and organic) illnesses.

Today, mental health professionals—medical and nonmedical— generally agree that the either/or understanding of mental illness as organic or functional is really both/and. Treating mental illness is not a choice between medication or talk therapy, but a choice of *what* therapies will best serve the person involved. Recovering from depression is a collaborative process between patient, physician, psychologist, spiritual director, family, and friends. Persons suffering from depression must have courage to face their depression. They must have patience. They must have help. A holistic approach is required in therapy because good therapy treats more than depression. It treats a person with depression. Attending to the needs of the whole person has always been the goal of good medicine, clinical psychology, and healthy religion. This is especially true in the treatment of depression.

The question is not whether we need therapy *or* salvation, healing *or* forgiveness. We need not be forced to choose between medication, psychotherapy, counseling, or faithful prayer. This is especially true when speaking of our health, where specialization is the norm. We go to medical doctors for our physical health. We go to psychiatrists, psychologists, therapists, or counselors for our mental health. We seek out pastors or priests, rabbis or new-age gurus to delve into our spiritual health. Specialization is important. There is value in knowing a lot about a little, instead of a little about a lot. But we can't be whole unless we understand ourselves, our relationships, and our world in an integrated manner. As pastor and physician, we invite you to enter into these conversations on depression with this integrated view of who you are as a person.

Words and Language

The common denominator of human discourse is words. Words form language. Different disciplines develop different words to create a language to talk about their subjects. Language can be off-putting. Sometimes it's intimidating. Sometimes it seems like snobbery or an affectation specifically designed to exclude the uninitiated. For some, the words *diabetes mellitus* are intimidating, and the words *carbohydrate metabolism* are snobbery. For others, the word *carburetor* is intimidating and the words *gear-ratio* are snobbery. Let's move past the language barriers that belong to medicine, religion, psychology, and sociology.

Medicine uses words like cerebrum and serotonin. Medical language is scientific, sounds a lot like Latin, and the community is The American Medical Association. Religion uses Greek words like *soteria* and *diakrisis*. God language has a theological flavor and those in the Christian religion call their community "church." In both communities, the search for truth is a quest for illumination—for a light to shine in the darkness. Perhaps there is only one truth—or light—at the heart of the universe, and we all glimpse it from our unique perspective.

In the common ground of the metaphysical—in science and theology—both disciplines can be mutually instructive. Light, in the gospel of John, is used as a metaphor for God. The physics of light holds a metaphor for religion. When ordinary light is projected through a prism, it's refracted into its component colors—red, green, blue, yellow, and so on. When the Light at the heart of the universe is projected through the cosmic prism toward our spinning planet, it's refracted into many hues based on our cultural legacy. A single color is all that most mortals are allowed to view. The Christian's cultural prism ingrains a bias toward belief in the God of the Bible. That doesn't exclude the authenticity of the vision of others of the human race whose cultural prism has provided them with a different wavelength of the Light. However, for Christians, the Bible—a story of power, poetry, and truth—discloses the Jesus of the gospels as the specific wavelength of Sovereign Light through which we might observe the great mysteries of life and death. The gospel story in its entirety must inform our faith, not just bits and pieces of it, and the whole of it is very complex. It's easy to know the bookends of Jesus' life. We embrace the nativity story with a sweet, self-satisfied sentimentality. We revel in the horrific, brutal, guilt-inducing details of his crucifixion. Too often, though, we have sanitized the blood, sweat, toil, and tears of the contradictory, chaotic, messy meat of his life. We have difficulty taking Jesus' choices and behavior seriously, with due regard for his words and actions that gave him his unique moral authority.

The instant we utter the word *God,* we are on the edge of language. We are conveyed immediately to the extremity of thought, the limits of comprehension, and the frontier of experience. We are exploring territory where the finite attempts to grasp the infinite. We come face to face with our human potential and our human limitations. Theology's task is daunting, not only because it engages both our mind and heart but also because it must connect with our experience. It is made more formidable by a religious culture in which God-talk is spewed out with such certainty. Impertinent. Insolent. Arrogant. Presuming to divulge God's secrets to people—complete and absolute. *God says...God does...God will...God won't...God doesn't...God thinks* ...God domesticated—part of the hired help—without reverence for the sacred Mystery. Both medicine and theology must stand hat in hand before the mysteries of their respective disciplines.

Whole persons don't section off their mind from their body, their psyche from their physiology, their personality from their society, or their character from their destiny. It helps to think about words (which influence our understanding, shape our experience, and define our existence) in the same way. Language must be integrated in ways that contribute to our wholeness. The different words in the language of medicine and theology often refer to the same or similar realities. When we speak of wholeness, hope, health, well-being, balance, healing, and salvation, are we speaking medically, psychologically, spiritually, or socially? The answer, of course, is all of the above, because words can be culturally cross-referenced to create bridges between the languages of human experience. The following cross-referenced word list does not have a "one-to-one" relationship, much less the same definitions, but is simply given as an example of vocabularies used in medicine and theology to speak of human experience.

Disease	Dis-ease
Mental illness	Sin
Psychosis	Guilt
Neurosis	Shame
Bipolar	Demon possession
Paranoia	Angst

Schizophrenia	Lost
Psychiatry	Gospel
Psychology	Forgiveness
Therapy	Salvation
Counseling	Pastoral care

Now, imagine a group of words in the middle ground.

Alienation
Despair
Anxiety
Melancholy
Disintegration
Confusion
Powerlessness
Healing
Health
Integration
Peace
Hope
Joy
Relief
Transformation

To emphasize, there isn't a one-to-one correlation between these words and the ones used in the two columns above. However, the middle-ground column helps us to see the relationship between language symbols describing human experience. It's important to use appropriate language to address appropriate issues. We must use the right tool for the right job. A hammer is not better than a saw. Each tool is appropriate to its task. However, to paraphrase Mark Twain, if all you bring to the workplace is a hammer, then every thing will be treated like a nail.

Health and Salvation

Several Greek words in the New Testament related to both health and salvation will help us understand this. *Sozo* or *soteria* are words related to save and salvation, and they speak of human wholeness, soundness, and safety. *Hugiaino* is the word for health. It means safe and sound. *Therapeuo* is the word for therapy. *Psyche* is the word for mind and *Psuche* is the word for soul. None of these words can be separated from *Soma*, the word for body. In the gospels there is a relationship between all these words as Jesus' ministry unfolds in compassionate healing, graceful forgiveness, powerful exorcisms, shaping a future vision, announcing the love of God, calling for just relationships, and affirming life over death. Jesus never spoke of the soul without caring for the body. A mature understanding of human experience is one in which such issues as health and salvation, mind and body, soul and spirit, pain and joy, hope and fear, anger and penitence, depression and despair coexist in a complex whole, rather than one in which they simply displace each other. In the areas of spiritual, mental, and physical health, everything must be integrated if we are to be whole persons.

This is especially true in our understanding of depression. Depression takes shape, expresses itself, and has consequences for human wholeness in terms of medicine, psychology, religion, social relationships, and culture. In our discussion of depression, we must not section off the person into various compartments, nor separate the person from culture and society. Physical, psychic, spiritual, and cultural conditions distort a person's sense of wholeness and well-being. All play a role in depression and block hope for a better future. Depression shouldn't be treated medically *or* psychologically *or* spiritually *or* socially. Good health is when the entire human organism—body, mind, spirit, and societal relationships—is in a state of well-being. The individual's humanity is at ease. Bad health is when the delicate balance in the entire human organism, or portions of it, has changed for the worse and the individual no longer has a sense of well-being. The individual's humanity is diseased. Disease can best be understood by separating it into prefix and suffix—*dis* and *ease*. Bad health—dis-ease—may be the inability to grasp a door handle, hear the telephone ring, make change for a dollar bill, or climb a flight of stairs without getting short of breath. Dis-ease may be clinical depression.

History, Stories, and Songs

Every person has a history and a life in time. Our history and our time line form our identity. We tell our story so others can know who we are. The stories others tell *about* us help us know who we are. Other people's stories not only tell us who *they* are but also help us understand who *we* are. We grew up on stories and songs.

We know stories of Jerusalem, Rome, London, and Los Angeles. We know stories of railroads and cattle drives. Stories of Valley Forge, Omaha Beach, and Iwo Jima. Of Vietnam, the peace movement, and civil rights. We know stories of Abraham, Esther, and John Mark.

There are stories of Joan of Arc, Florence Nightingale, Wyatt Earp, and Audie Murphy. Of Alexander the Great, Michelangelo, Martin Luther, Hamlet, Columbus, Thomas Jefferson, Winston Churchill, Willie Mays, Gandhi, Abe Lincoln, Dietrich Bonhoeffer, and Martin Luther King, Jr. There are stories closer to home of Grandma and Grandpa and uncles and aunts. We also know the songs. Cowboy songs, patriotic songs, country and western, pop, and gospel hymns. And opera, folk songs, and rock-and-roll. Also symphonies, string quartets, brass bands, blues, bluegrass, and jazz.

However, each of us is unique. We are not Everyman, or any man or any woman. We have names. Our stories unfold in distinct historical settings and connect with a particular cast of characters. The stories we tell and the songs we sing establish our place in the universe. They create the scaffold on which we order our lives. They provide a series of checks and balances for behavior. They assist in measuring reality. They provide a pathway and a vision. We must decide which are our stories and which are our songs. Further, we need to affirm which stories and songs are indispensable. Indispensable stories might be Bible stories and Babe Ruth. Galileo and Gettysburg. The stories of Thomas Edison and Rosa Parks. Family stories and Aesop's fables. There are stories that are entertaining and may even have purpose, but which aren't indispensable. Examples might be *Jack and the Beanstalk*, *The Glass Menagerie*, tales of John Dillinger and Madonna. Indispensable songs might be "My Country, 'Tis of Thee," "Battle Hymn of the Republic," "Streets of Laredo," "Danny Boy," and "Amazing Grace." Songs resonant with meaning, but which aren't indispensable might be "Shenandoah," "White Christmas," and "Heartbreak Hotel."

Stories and songs bring us blessing, peace, hope, grace, joy, love, faithfulness, fidelity, and liberation. They also pummel us with despair, betrayal, faithlessness, infidelity, failure, sorrow, perfidy, carnality, upheaval, war, conquest, captivity, oppression, and guilt. We are riveted by lives lived out in the cut and thrust of day-to-day existence. Lives that are messy, chaotic, confusing, terrifying, lonely, painful, sinful, blessed, beautiful, and joyous. Just like ours. Our experience tells us that our lives mirror the mix, mayhem, mystery, and magical enchantment of those stories and songs.

We are not blank slates when we are born. We are forever influenced at conception by the genetic material scientists call DNA. We were deeply marked at birth by the health of our mother (or lack of it) during pregnancy, and subsequently by our nuclear family, our extended family, our geography, by childhood peers, teachers and preachers of our youth, by friends and enemies, by race, nationality, economics, world setting, and our church.

We were also polluted by what theologians call The Fall. The Bible stories, from Genesis to Revelation, as morality tales, are mixed—that is to say, human—and are complex and messy. The Bible story resonates in our hearts and minds with a ring of truth, but we believe it because we choose to. Faith is a celebration of life's confusion and messiness. Baptism washes away our sins, but it doesn't make us blank slates. Thus, marked at birth and by all of the experiences that followed, and marked by our humanity in The Fall, the Bible stories are both universal and personal. They tell our story. They tell us where we came from, who we are, and where we are going. There is purpose in our world.

Like Adam and Eve, we have been created by God, somehow in God's image, and we dream of immortality. Like Adam and Eve, we possess all the strengths and weaknesses of human flesh. Like Adam and Eve, we had our own garden eastward in Eden. We are bone of each other's bone, and flesh of each other's flesh. We confronted God in our garden, walking with God in the cool of the evening. There was a serpent in our garden, and we have known temptation. There was a tree of knowledge of good and evil in our garden, and we have known both good and evil. We have fallen from grace in our garden, and an angel with a flaming sword has driven us from paradise and stands guard at our garden's gate. There are places to which we can never return, places that are closed to us forever. We are alienated from ourselves, from others, and from God. We have learned that we are keepers of our brothers and sisters, and we know that we shall surely die.

The Framework of Time

We human beings not only have history—stories and songs—but also have time on our hands. It can be purposeful time, wasted time, painful time, healing time, damned time, or fulfilling time, and our days usually contain some of all of it. We have a feeling we are running out of time. We have a past to make sense of, a present in which to live, and a future to face. All the frameworks of time (past, present, and future) are emotionally laden—burdensome or freeing, threatening or hopeful, haunting or comforting, sickening or healing. We live and breathe, are happy and sad, hopeful and regretful, we suffer and celebrate. We experience life through our bodies, intellects, and emotions. We experience life in relationships and in a culture, and we experience it in ways that lie beyond explanation–in terms of the spiritual, the mysterious, and the numinous. "There are more things in heaven and earth, Horatio," Shakespeare wrote in *Hamlet,* "than are dreamt of in your philosophy."

Rubem Alves, the Brazilian philosopher, theologian, and poet, is fond of saying, "Hope is to hear the music of the future, faith is to dance it." To do so, we must be able to *hear* the music and we must be able to *dance.*

The breath of life, O Lord, seems spent.
My body is tense, my mind filled with anxiety,
Yet I have no zest, no energy.
I am helpless to allay my fears,
I am incapable of relaxing my limbs.
Dark thoughts constantly invade my head,
And I have no power over them.
Was ever an oak tree buffeted by wind,
As the gales of melancholy now buffet my soul?
Was ever a ship tossed by the waves,
As my soul is now tossed by misery?
Did ever the foundation of a house crumble,
As my own life now crumbles to dust?
Friends no longer want to visit me.
You have driven away my spiritual brethren.
I am now outcast from your church.
No longer the flowers want to bloom for me.
No longer the trees come into leaf for me.
No longer the birds sing at my window.
My fellow Christians condemn me as an idle sinner.
Lord, raise up my soul, revive my body.[2]

Gregory of Nazianzus (329–389), Theologian and Preacher,
Cappadocian Father, Bishop of Constantinople

---

[2] *The HarperCollins Book of Prayers,* comp. Robert Van de Weyer (Edison, N.J.: Castle Books, 1997), 176–77.

The Man Who Couldn't Dance: PART TWO

Ernest stopped for coffee in the lobby of his office building. The board meeting had gone well. They would be able to fulfill their obligations for another six months at least. He carried his mocha across a marble floor, under a vaulted canopy of steel and glass, open and sunlit, with potted trees and flowering shrubs providing shade and scent. He chose an empty table and sipped his coffee, but he listened with growing irritation to the cell-phone conversation from a nearby table. Tom was in finance. A friend and colleague for fifteen years, Tom blathered on about amortizing some loan. "No," Tom said, "I'm not a genius. A genius is someone like Edward Einstein."

Ernest turned to look. Tom was as serious as death. Unbelievable. The humor of it was lost on Ernest. Just unbelievable! The ignorance of people never ceased to amaze him. Seething, he pushed away his half-finished coffee. Finally, the phone piped its exasperating, musical good-bye. "Tom, can I ask you a question?"

"Sure."

"Is that thing an electronic device or a tin can on a string?"

"What's your point?"

"Do you have to yell?"

Tom shrugged. "I speak up to make sure they understand me."

"Then take your personal business outside."

"Ernie, this is a public place."

"That's why you don't shout your conversations into it."

Tom frowned and headed for the elevator.

Ernest stalked him. "At least talk about something interesting."

Tom pressed the button for the eighteenth floor.

"Make a date with your girlfriend or something. You're boring."

Tom followed Ernest into his office. He tried to be agreeable. "Are you okay? How's Mary? the kids? How come you're so angry?"

Ernest snorted, "It's *Albert* Einstein, you moron!"

The conversation turned edgy. "What the hell's the matter with you? You were the go-to guy. Now you're moody. You let things fall through the cracks."

"If you make CEO before I do," Ernest said, "then talk to me."

The conversation ended ugly. "Don't talk to me about girlfriends or affairs, you sad bastard! I know you dip your pen in the company ink!"

Ernest picked up a memo. "Don't let the door hit you in the back on the way out."

17

CHAPTER TWO

The Physical Disease

The whole head is sick,
and the whole heart faint.
From the sole of the foot even to the head,
there is no soundness in it,
but bruises and sores
and bleeding wounds;
they have not been drained, or bound up,
or softened with oil.

ISAIAH 1:5–6

"The eye is the lamp of the body. So, if your eye is healthy, your
whole body will be full of light; but if your eye is unhealthy, your
whole body will be full of darkness. If then the light in you is
darkness, how great is the darkness!"

MATTHEW 6:22–23

Life is not fair. The random association of genes at conception encodes people for biological characteristics, including mental and physical diseases. People may be crippled by the simple process of being birthed. People begin life at different points of entry into the geographic, societal, and cultural global environment. Some have more resources than others: wealth, position, intelligence, courage, stamina, strength, speed, fast-twitch muscles, and eye-hand coordination. Every person is wounded by family, friend, and foe. Every person is victimized in some way and to some degree. No one gets out of life unscathed. No one ends life without regrets. However, no one single thing causes any one single thing. Character is malleable. Genetics and circumstances are not absolute destiny. One person may clearly be less fortunate than another, but we need not wallow in our victimization. People can move on. People make choices, plans, and progress. That is the defining characteristic of being human.

One of life's unfair circumstances is having a depressive illness. What do we know about depression in American life?

Statistics on Depression

■ Almost twenty million Americans (about 10 percent of the population) are clinically depressed in any given year, establishing depression as one of the major causes of medical disability in this country.

■ One percent of Americans suffer from manic-depression (bipolar disorder).

■ Manic-depression affects men and women equally.

■ Persons of lower socioeconomic status (especially women) have a higher incidence of depression.

■ Victims of racial prejudice, per se, do not suffer higher rates of depression.

■ Sixty percent of smokers have undergone an episode of major depression, compared with only 10 percent of the general population.

■ Eating disorders (anorexia, bulimia, binging/purging) are linked to depression. Forty percent of young American females (compared to 10 percent of young American males) have some form of eating disorder.

■ Destructive behaviors (compulsive gambling, shoplifting, drug and alcohol addiction, and sexual behavior) are statistically linked with depression.

■ Physical or sexual abuse during childhood increases the risk of depression, especially in women.

■ Twice as many women as men develop depression.

■ After childbirth, the postpartum mother is at greater risk for depression.

■ Married, single, divorced, or widowed women have the same rates of depression.

■ Married men have a lower incidence of depression than single, divorced, or widowed men.

- Depression affects children and adolescents, although it is less common in children (and perhaps more difficult to recognize).

- The incidence of depression in male and female children is identical.

- At puberty, the rates of depression in both boys and girls go up.

- After girls begin their menses, the rate of depression among adolescent girls is twice that of adolescent boys (i.e., identical to the ratio of adult women to men).

- The biggest factor for depression in children appears to be genetic—a family history of depression.

- Identical twins separated at birth, in spite of separate and unique environments, are more than twice as likely to have depression or manic-depression than the general population.

- Children of a parent with depression have a 10 percent greater risk of developing this disorder compared to the general population.

- Children of a parent with manic-depression have a one to two percent greater risk of developing manic-depression compared with the general population.

- The onset of severe depression in childhood and adolescence is associated with more severe or recurrent bouts of depression in adult life.

- Depression affects the elderly, but aging in and of itself does not cause depression.

- Not quite one percent of Americans sixty-five years of age and older experience clinical depression. (These statistics are difficult to evaluate, because this age group suffers more from chronic disease, may have experienced the loss of a spouse, or may be confined in long-term care facilities. But skilled therapists can tell the difference between bereavement and depression.)

- Patients with depression are up to four times more likely to have a heart attack over a period of time than the non-depressed. (Health issues that increase the risk of heart attack such as smoking, weight, amount of exercise, cholesterol and estrogen levels, and medications have been factored in to these statistical studies.)

- Depression is as strong an independent risk factor for heart disease as elevated cholesterol.

■ The statistical link between heart attack and depression is as strong as the link between heart attack and smoking.

■ Heart attack per se doesn't cause clinical depression.

■ Depressed patients are more likely to die from a heart attack than the non-depressed (comparison studies with similar degrees of heart damage).

■ Patients with cancer, diabetes, epilepsy, and osteoporosis have a higher risk of disability and premature death if they are clinically depressed.

■ People with migraine are three times more likely to have depression than people who don't experience migraine.

■ Patients with certain neurological diseases such as stroke and Parkinson's disease have a greater incidence of depression (as distinct from sadness at experiencing a health catastrophe).

■ Some 40 percent of stroke victims develop clinical depression.

■ MRI scans reveal that strokes affecting the left frontal lobe caused the highest incidence of depression, while strokes affecting the right frontal lobe caused the lowest incidence.

■ Depression after left frontal lobe strokes is immediate and more profound, but depression developed more slowly and was less severe in patients with right frontal lobe strokes.

■ Electrical stimulation in the left frontal lobe of non-depressed test subjects produced feelings of depression. When the electrical stimulation was stopped, the feelings of depression disappeared within ninety seconds. Electrical stimulation of the right frontal lobe in test subjects didn't produce feelings of depression.

■ Thirty thousand Americans commit suicide each year and depression, manic-depression, and/or alcohol are associated with about 80 percent of these deaths.

What are we to make of this slew of statistics? To begin with, they don't explain depression. Explanations must be sought in other disciplines: natural science, social science, culture, anthropology, mythology, intuition, and reflection. There are as many theories to explain the statistics as there are statistics. Pundits are left stewing in a brew of nature and nurture, but natural science favors nature as the fundamental cause.

Diagnosis of Depression

When you ask a friend how she's doing, she might say, "I'm depressed." When a psychiatrist asks a colleague what's wrong with a particular patient, the psychiatrist might say, "She's depressed." Your friend means she's temporarily down. The psychiatrist means the patient has depressive illness. What's the difference?

In 1952, the American Psychiatric Association first published the *Diagnostic and Statistical Manual of Mental Disorders* to establish criteria for diagnosing mental illness. The DSM has gone through four revisions, the latest being 1994, and is referred to as DSM-IV. (A fifth revision is being prepared for publication in 2010.) The *Manual* is obviously not carved in stone, nor does it meet with complete approval by all therapists. Nevertheless, it is an attempt to standardize the classification of mental illness and provide a point of departure for understanding and communication. Classification constructs a framework for research and sets forth the criteria for diagnosis. Without an accurate diagnosis, it is impossible to choose appropriate therapies or to predict the outcome of the illness.

Physicians diagnose physical illness based on the patient's history and symptoms (story), physical examination (physical signs), and objective laboratory data (blood tests, urine tests, cultures, X-rays, biopsies, etc.). Physicians diagnose depression by the patient's story and behavior, critiquing them with finely honed clinical skills. It's a subjective diagnosis. To date, there are no laboratory tests that can accurately and unfailingly make a diagnosis of mental illness, though there may be such tests someday. A trained, clinical health professional can reasonably make a diagnosis of depression based on the criteria in DSM-IV.

The Diagnostic and Statistical Manual-IV identifies ten mood disorders (sometimes referred to now as affective disorders) and sets forth the criteria for their diagnosis.[1] Among these ten disorders are

---

[1]DSM-IV recognizes postpartum depression (PPD) and seasonal affective disorder (SAD) as unique syndromes, but it doesn't list them as separate categories of mood disorders. They are included as subsets to one of the other major classifications of mood disorder. PPD occurs following pregnancy (although not every pregnancy) and ranges from mild to severe. Rarely, psychotic episodes with delusions and hallucinations occur. Although linked in some way to dramatic reductions in estrogen and progesterone following delivery, all pregnant women have this same reduction in hormones but not all have depression, so other factors must play a role. A previous episode of major depression is a known risk for PPD. Women who experience postpartum depression have an increased incidence of major depression later in life. SAD is characterized by depression at seasons of the year with less sunshine and shorter days. The depression can be mild or severe and can even include suicidal thoughts.

episodes of depression and mania (alone and in varying combinations, degrees of severity, and length of time of the mood change), as well as mood changes secondary to medical conditions and substance abuse. For our purpose (and simplicity) we will identify five clearly defined, common mood disorders detailed in DSM-IV:

Major Depressive Disorder (Unipolar Disorder)

■ A mood disorder defined as five or more of the following symptoms (present for at least two weeks and not caused by medical conditions) including one or both of the first two.

■ Depressed mood such as sadness, pessimism, anxiety, apathy, numbness (in teenagers and children the overriding mood may be irritability or anger).

■ Diminished interest or pleasure in all or most activities.

■ Changes in appetite, weight gain or loss, including eating disorders such as binging, anorexia, purging, and bulimia.

■ Sleep disorders, which can include insomnia or prolonged sleeping.

■ Restlessness or sluggish body movements.

■ Fatigue or loss of vitality and energy.

■ Feelings of inappropriate guilt and worthlessness.

■ Diminished ability to think, concentrate, and make decisions.

■ Recurrent thoughts of death and/or suicide.

Manic-Depression (Bipolar Disorder I)

■ A mixed mood disorder defined as periods of normal mood with alternating episodes of depression or mania (not due to medical condition or drugs). Either phase may last weeks, months, or years. Mania demonstrates at least three of the following over a period of at least one week with symptoms sufficiently severe to cause marked impairment at work or in relationships or to necessitate hospitalization:

■ Auto-intoxication, which fuels an inflated self-esteem with hyper-elevated mood, over-the-top elation, exuberance, and grandiosity.

■ Frenzied periods of activity.

■ Decreased need for sleep.

■ High-speed talk and an almost irrepressible impulse to keep talking.

■ Rapid thinking (flight of ideas or feeling that thoughts are racing).

■ Initiating flamboyant and extravagant projects.

■ Involvement in wild escapades (sexual activities or business deals that are risky and have a high potential for painful consequences) with no thought of failure and no sense of boundaries.

■ Spending sprees, maxing out credit cards, and using up savings.

■ Poor judgment.

■ When the manic episode ends, these patients return to a normal or depressed mode. (See signs and symptoms of depression.)

Hypomania (Bipolar Disorder II)

Mania in Bipolar II is diagnosed by the same criteria for Bipolar Disorder I, but the symptoms and behavior are milder in degree. The low-grade elevated mood goes on for long periods of time and doesn't *alternate* with periods of depression, although the patient may still have one or more major depressive episodes.

Dysthymic Disorder

Dysthymic disorder is a chronic, smoldering depression with symptoms similar to major depressive disorder but milder in degree. The depression is long-lasting rather than episodic, with symptoms persisting for two years or more. Patients may be symptom-free for up to two months. The diagnosis is not made if the patient has ever had a manic or hypomanic episode. Furthermore, the condition is not due to medical condition, drugs, or bereavement. The diagnostic criteria, while depressed, include two (or more) of the following:

■ Poor appetite or overeating.

■ Lack of sleep or excessive sleep.

■ Low energy and fatigue.

■ Low self-esteem.

■ Poor concentration or difficulty making decisions.

■ Feelings of hopelessness.

Cyclothymic Disorder (CD)

CD is characterized by two years of inexplicable changes of mood from highs to lows on a day-to-day basis that don't meet the criteria for a manic or depressive episode.

DSM-IV recognizes that depression can be a component of medical illnesses, and conversely, that depression can mimic many physical diseases. Researchers believe the depression in certain diseases is an integral part of the physical illness, not an emotional response to being sick or facing death. Some of these diseases are rare, some are common (some carry the names of the doctors who first described them). Such illnesses include adrenal insufficiency (Addison's Disease), adrenal hypersufficiency (Cushings syndrome), diabetes, hypothyroidism, hepatitis, HIV, third stage syphilis, brain cancer, lung cancer, dementia in the elderly, multiple sclerosis, Parkinson's disease, stroke, and lupus erythematosus among others. Furthermore, there are two relatively obscure and vague disorders (chronic fatigue syndrome and fibromyalgia), whose diagnosis is made by a constellation of symptoms in the general absence of objective diagnostic tests, just as in depression. To add to the confusion, these diseases are often treated by anti-depressant medication. The actual existence of CFS and fibromyalgia as distinct diseases is debated in some quarters.

The occurrence of depression as part of certain physical illnesses (requiring therapy targeting the physical illness) is why medical doctors must do a thorough physical examination before ascribing depression solely to an illness of the brain (with therapy targeting a mental illness). Accuracy in diagnosis, both of physical and mental diseases, is especially important because manic-depression (Bipolar Disorder I) requires different therapy than depression (Unipolar Disorder).

Science and Depression

Despite advances in the sciences that have bearing on the cause and treatment of depression, it is fair to say that what we know is miniscule when compared to what we don't know. The brain is a marvelous three pounds of gray and white matter that contains one hundred billion neurons, one trillion supporting cells, and various chemicals and hormones. It is largely unexplored territory. Research on the brain is at the approximate location of Lewis and Clark in their base camp in St. Louis before they started their exploration of the Northwest Territories.

The history of progress in medicine is long and tortuous. It meandered through the ancient cultures of both East and West and was practiced by shamans, medicine men, mystics, priests, seers, and even barbers before finally linking up with the scientific method. Over the millennia, the tools of medicine have ranged from bird entrails to electrons. The fathers of modern Western medicine are Hippocrates (Greece, ca. 400 B.C.E.) and Claudius Galen (Rome, ca. C.E. 180). Perhaps the most important contribution of Hippocrates was his observation, "Life is short; the Art is long." That insight should give pause to anyone making ironclad pronouncements from the vantage point of his or her respective discipline. Too often, both scientist and theologian are arrogant about their dogma. Learning is a process, not a product. Knowledge must be embraced with humility, fully aware of the gulf between knowledge and certainty.

Galen made a stab at physiology in his explanation that disease states were caused by an imbalance in the four body "humours" (mucous, phlegm, black bile, and yellow bile). This explanation is considered quaint in light of two millennia of scientific advances, but both he and Aristotle considered depression (what they called melancholia) a physical illness. During the Middle Ages, the idea of depression as a physical illness was abandoned as clerics gained more power and redefined mental illness in moral terms. Those who suffered from mental illness were considered possessed by demons. Diseases of the mind changed from physical illnesses to sin. The diagnosis of mental illness has yet to recover from the twin stigmas of demon possession and sin.

Galen's paradigm of disease theory held general sway in the Western world until the scientific explosion between the seventeenth and twentieth centuries. William Harvey was an English physician who demonstrated the circulation of the blood in 1628. John Hunter was an English surgeon who robbed graves and dissected corpses and is given credit for establishing the sciences of anatomy and pathology in the 1750s. Samuel Guthrie, an American, invented chloroform in 1831 and made painless surgery possible through general anesthesia. The Augustinian monk, Gregor Johann Mendel, founded the science of genetics in 1866 through his observations on peas growing in his garden. Doctor Simmelweiss demonstrated "contagion" on the obstetrical wards in Vienna and dramatically reduced infection rates by simply washing his hands between patients. Wilhelm Roentgen discovered X-rays in 1895 and Pierre and Marie Curie discovered radium in 1898, making it possible to "see" inside the body. In 1928, Alexander Fleming discovered penicillin (although its practical use as an antibiotic was not established until 1940) and together with Gerhard Domagk's discovery of sulfa in 1935, antisepsis and the curing of infection was possible. During those centuries, the study of mental illness was rooted in the discoveries of the scientific method.

Medicine of the mind (psychiatry) took a detour when Sigmund Freud (in 1895 and the years following) looked at mental illness in an entirely different way. A genius of observation and insight, he believed mental illness was the result of unconscious conflict. He devised a vocabulary to talk about such problems (Ego, Superego, Id, Oedipus Complex, Electra Complex), and attributed depressive illness to anger turned against one's self. The treatment Freud prescribed was psychoanalysis so the patient could bring conflicts into their consciousness and get well. Freud essentially took psychiatry out of the mainstream of scientific medicine (anatomy, genetics, pharmacology, endocrinology, and epidemiology) for almost a half century. The crux of his work is still debated among health professionals, but there is no doubt he had a profound influence on the understanding and treatment of mental illnesses that lasts to this day. Moreover, not to disparage classic Freudian psychoanalysis, because delving into our subconscious to probe conflict and understand motive is still a useful insight, but even Freud said, "Sometimes a cigar is just a cigar." In 1907, the Russian scientist, Ivan Pavlov, began his studies that demonstrated he could cause dogs to salivate after appropriate "conditioning" when stimulated with food and/or a ringing bell. Behavioral science was born and rats-in-a-maze and other techniques contributed to our understanding of how the mind worked.

At the dawn of the twentieth century, standing on the shoulders of the giants of thought, observation, and physical research, the modern sciences of anatomy, chemistry, pharmacology, genetics, epidemiology, endocrinology, physics, and engineering took front and center. Great progress has been made in unlocking some of the secrets of the brain and mental illness. With the cautionary mantra of all good scientists—"pending further research," the following approximates our current understanding of depression.

How Do We Know What We Think We Know about Depression?

There are six sciences involved in research into depression, though they clearly overlap. For example, where does anatomy end and pharmacology or endocrinology begin? However, for purpose of discussion, the six sciences are anatomy, neuropharmacology, genetics, endocrinology, engineering, and epidemiology. I would like to add a seventh science—serendipity—though not technically a science. Serendipity (happy accidents plus astute observation) has moved science along the path of discovery in many fields, to name three:

the discovery of penicillin by Fleming, the discovery of the North American continent by Columbus or the Vikings (depending on your reading of history and your ethnicity), and the discovery of radiation by Roentgen. Serendipity has certainly contributed to our understanding of depression and mental illness, particularly in elucidating how certain drugs affect the brain and what happens to people when strokes or accidents injure a part of the brain.

Brain Anatomy and Depression

Anatomists have been dissecting brains for centuries. They described its various parts (cerebrum, cerebellum, etc.) and noted that some of the tissue was gray matter and some was white matter. Finding and naming the chunks of the brain is called gross anatomy, not because it was "yucky," but because the chunks were large.

The Cerebrum. The cerebrum is the outer covering of four-fifths of the brain and its folded appearance makes it look like a cauliflower. The outer coating of the cerebrum is gray in color (gray matter) and is called the cerebral cortex. The cerebral cortex contains the nerve cell bodies (the neurons). Beneath the cerebral cortex is a white colored substance (white matter) that contains the nerve fibers (axons) that transmit the messages between the neuron and other nerve centers in the brain and spinal cord. The cerebrum is divided into two halves, the right and left cerebral hemisphere. Most nerves cross from one side to the other in the neck, so that the left cerebral hemisphere controls the right side of the body and the right cerebral hemisphere controls the left side of the body. The cerebrum has specialized areas that interpret information from the five senses (sight, smell, hearing, taste, and touch), program thought, and initiate voluntary movement through muscle stimulation.

The Frontal Lobes of the Cerebral Cortex. The prefrontal cortex is located along the front rim of the cerebrum. It controls rationality, concentration, planning, envisioning the future, problem solving, and multi-tasking. The prefrontal cortex is the area of the brain that makes humans human.

The Sensory Cortex. The sensory cortex is located along the rear rim of the cerebral cortex. It receives sensory information from the thalamus and works in concert with the prefrontal cortex to interpret and act on incoming stimuli. It helps distinguish genuine threats from the environment from false alarms.

The Motor Cortex. The motor cortex lies along both sides of the cerebrum and contains the neurons that send the signals to the muscles that control voluntary movement. Scientists have mapped which areas of the motor cortex control which muscles. One of the curious findings is that the area that controls the thumb is extraordinarily large in comparison to other motor areas. The opposable thumb elevated humankind to the position of toolmaker and user.

The Cerebellum. The cerebellum (meaning "little brain") is a small round mass of tissue that is nestled under the cerebral hemispheres at the rear of the brain, and it sits atop the midbrain. It

BRAIN BISECTION

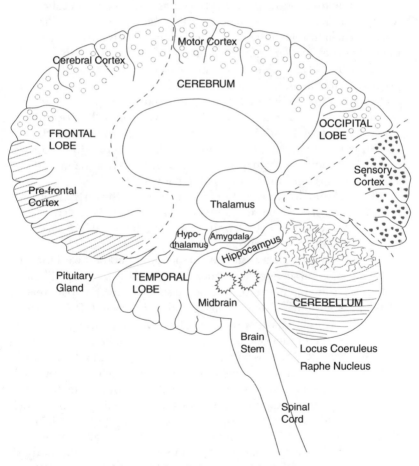

Bisection shows the major functioning areas of the brain.

coordinates learning and controls complicated functions of balance by gauging the spatial relationship of various parts of the body in relation to the whole body. The cerebellum compares what you intended to do (a command from the motor cortex in the cerebrum) to what you are actually doing. It fine-tunes these movements on a moment-to-moment basis through intricate feedback mechanisms that act as both brake and throttle. The cerebellum is responsible for motor skills such as riding a bicycle or walking a fence rail.

The Midbrain. The midbrain lies deep in the center of the brain and has nerve tracts that connect the thalamus and cerebrum with the spinal cord. A cluster of neurons located in the midbrain (termed the *raphe nucleus*) secrete a chemical called serotonin. Another cluster of midbrain neurons (termed the *locus coeruleus*) secrete a chemical called norepinephrine. These neuronal production centers receive stimuli from the amygdala to release their chemicals and they are dispersed up to the higher brain centers and down the spinal cord to the body.

The Thalamus. The thalamus sits atop the amygdala and processes information from the eye and the ear (sight and sound) and routes it first to the amygdala and then to the cognitive parts of the brain in the prefrontal and sensory cortexes and the hippocampus. The nose and tactile senses (odor and touch) are routed directly to the amygdala, bypassing the thalamus. Odors may provide stronger feelings and memories than sight and sound, having been bathed selectively in the primitive juices of the amygdala.

The Hypothalamus. Located in the midbrain below the thalamus, the hypothalamus is involved in appetite, sex drive, and sleep. It produces corticotropin releasing factor (CRF), which influences endocrine function.

The Pituitary Gland. Situated in the lower part of the midbrain, the pituitary gland secretes hormones that are critical for the endocrine system (thyroid, parathyroid, adrenals, testes, ovaries, and pancreatic islets of Langerhans). The pituitary gland responds to CRF secreted by the hypothalamus to produce adrenocorticotropic hormone (ACTH), which influences the adrenal gland to make cortisol.

The Amygdala. The amygdala got its name from a Latin word that describes the shape of an almond, and it is located at the base of the brain. Although very small, it is central to brain function. In evolutionary terms, the amygdala was the functioning brain of the crocodile and pit viper. It triggers vegetative responses (licking, chewing, rooting) and produces primitive emotions (fear, rage, anger, aggression). The amygdala is the command center for the body's reaction to threat (real or perceived). It is hard-wired. When stimulated, it doesn't wait for instructions from the frontal lobes of the cerebral cortex, but instantaneously sounds the alarm (Klaxons and flashing red lights). In a lightning-like chain reaction, it jolts the hypothalamus, the pituitary gland, and the adrenals: The body is flushed in cortisol, epinephrine, and norepinephrine. The heart pounds, the pulse races, the lungs inflate, the pupils widen, arteries to the muscles expand, and a surge of sugar (fuel) is blasted into the system. At the same time, all nonessential services—stomach, bowel, kidney, sex drive, and immune system—are shut down (sometimes bowel and bladder are involuntarily evacuated). The amygdala, to use a phrase from the Old West, "shoots first and asks questions later." When the amygdala is stimulated in animals, it produces rage. When it is removed from animals, they become docile. The amygdala receives stimuli from both the prefrontal cerebral cortex and the sensory cortex, the areas of the brain where the human organism distinguishes genuine threats from false alarms. These higher centers can apply the brakes to the amygdala if they don't deem the threat to be significant. This control mechanism sometimes functions poorly. The amygdala is believed to play a role in psychoses, mania, and depression. The amygdala also helps form long-term memories, which is why early memories may be tinged with profound emotions.

The Hippocampus. The hippocampus is located in the cerebrum's temporal lobes. Its name came from the Greek word for seahorse, which, with imagination, this part of the brain resembles. The hippocampus receives messages from the amygdala, integrates the sensory stimuli into the sensory and prefrontal cortices, and helps evaluate them in the context of previous experiences. The hippocampus also functions in spatial orientation, constructing three-dimensional "mental-maps" of the body in relationship to where its "place" is in its "space." Damage to the hippocampus (stroke victims) makes it difficult for the person to navigate in what would normally be familiar territory. The hippocampus processes and stores short-term memories before transferring them to the cerebral cortex for permanent storage. Again, since the information passed through the amygdala, it soaks up primitive emotions that may remain attached to long-term memories held in the cerebral cortex. Damage to the hippocampus makes it difficult to form new, short-term memories, but the person still has access to long-term memories in the cerebral cortex.

The Brain Stem. The brain stem gathers up all of the nerve fibers streaming out of the cerebrum, cerebellum, thalamus, and midbrain and acts as a conduit to connect them to the spinal cord.

The Neuron. After the big chunks of the brain were identified, scientists set about to identify the tiniest fragments. Using tools such as the microscope and electron microscope, and joining forces with organic chemists, enzyme chemists, and immunologists, the field of cellular biology was born and a single cell was identified as the basic functioning unit of the brain. Called a neuron, this cell has a nucleus (its own brain), a few short appendages called dendrites with receptors (eyes and ears) to receive messages from other neurons, and a long axon (arm and hand) that reaches out to neurons in other parts of the brain to give it/them messages. It passes along the message with chemicals called neurotransmitters. This subject will be further discussed in the following section on neuropharmacology. Neurons have dedicated tasks—sight, hearing, smell, touch, taste, motion, cognition, memory, balance, spatial perceptions, hormone production, and creating emotions. The approximately 100 billion neurons in the brain are all connected to each other like a vast mainframe computer. Like a computer, the cells are either "on" or "off" and all communication is a two-way process. That is, each neuron both gives and receives information in performing its unique task.

Neuropharmacology and Depression

Neuropharmacology is the science of what chemicals affect brain function and how they do it. Science has learned that a neuron doesn't communicate with another neuron by "touching" it with its axon. There is a gap (synapse) between the neuron's axon and the neighboring neuron. Communication is done by various chemicals (neurotransmitters). Without neurotransmitters, the brain doesn't work. It can't communicate with itself, and it can't send messages to the rest of the body. When a neuron is stimulated, an electrical impulse passes down its axon. At the end of the axon are containers (vesicles) filled with neurotransmitters that are released by the electrical impulse. The neurotransmitters flow into the gap (synapse) between the axon and the next neuron and bind to a protein (receptor site) in the dendrites of the second neuron. This switches that neuron "on" or "off" to perform its function. Each neurotransmitter has a unique receptor site in the dendrites of other neurons. After the receptor site has received the message, it releases the neurotransmitter back into the gap (synapse). The axon of the first neuron "takes back" the chemical (a reuptake process) that it released to send the message in the first place, or, in some cases, enzymes in the gap (synapse) break down the neurotransmitter.

Several different neurotransmitters have been discovered. One is serotonin and another is norepinephrine (produced respectively, as we have seen, by neuron clusters in the raphe nucleus and locus coeruleus of the midbrain). A third chemical, dopamine, also acts as a neurotransmitter, and there are probably many others yet to be identified. When the various neurotransmitters are released at the ends of axons and picked up by the receptor sites of their target neurons, every part of the brain (cerebrum, cerebellum, thalamus, hypothalamus, hippocampus, midbrain, and brain stem) is influenced

THE NEURON

The neuron, a single cell, is the basic functioning unit of the brain.

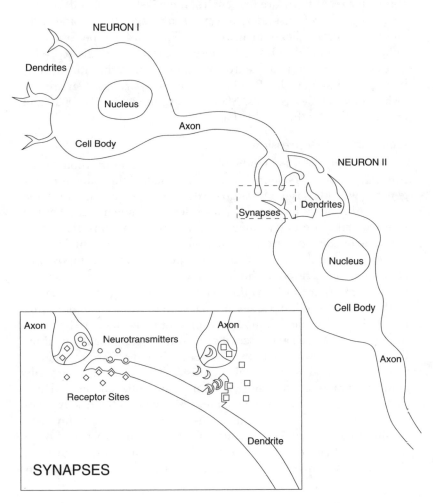

to produce a coordinated response. This makes many things possible: not only stirring sugar into tea, reading, running the 100-meter hurdles, flying a supersonic airplane, painting a picture, feeling joy, experiencing sorrow, making love, responding to a noise in the night, fighting to protect your family, and running for your life; but also apathy, depression, mania, delusions, hallucinations, seizures, diabetes, psoriasis, and murderous rage.

The system is complex beyond comprehension. Neurons may communicate with a single neuron or with innumerable neurons. The result is a finely tuned, coordinated cascade of responses within the brain that creates purposeful human actions and emotions. A useful metaphor is to picture the functions of a symphony orchestra. The conductor reads the score (the environmental stimulus) and uses his baton (the neurotransmitter) to send a message to each musician (another neuron), singly or in concert. The musician performs the unique task allotted to his or her instrument based on the score for that specific instrument (neuron function). An orchestral piece is produced that may be Beethoven's *Fifth Symphony,* Gershwin's "Rhapsody in Blue," Sousa's "Stars and Stripes Forever," or Flatt and Scruggs's "Under the Double Eagle."

Genetics and Depression

As noted, Gregor Mendel, the nineteenth-century monk who, ironically, failed his science exams in school, laid the foundation for genetics with his observations on garden peas. In the years since, the science of genetics has made great strides. It is known that inherited characteristics are determined by structures known as genes that combine in pairs (one from the male and one from the female of the species) at conception. Each gene is a protein that is composed of combinations of three of the following four amino acids: adenine, guanine, cytosine, and thymine. The particular sequence of amino acids is called a codon. Genes are made up of strings of codons that create the DNA that is bound in a spiral of pairs characterized as a double helix—a peek at the secret of life—which earned a Nobel Prize for James Watson and Francis Crick. DNA dictates the genetic framework for the biological organism. Scientists have virtually completed mapping the entire human genome—the codons in DNA that makes us who and what we are. This includes the discovery of genes and their location in the double helix that are involved in producing certain diseases (asthma, psoriasis, and diabetes), though it is doubtful that *one* gene is the cause of any *one* thing. Most geneticists think that multiple genes acting in concert are responsible for depression. It may be that certain genes "bend the twig" toward certain diseases when the "tree" is mature, establishing thresholds of vulnerability (high, medium, or low). The closer we are on the family tree to a relative with depression—a depressed mother instead of a depressed aunt—the greater the likelihood of depression.

Endocrinology and Depression

The endocrine system is made up of a set of glandular organs that include the pituitary, thyroid, parathyroid, adrenals, ovaries, testes, and the pancreatic islets of Langerhans. These glands produce complex chemicals called hormones that are released into the bloodstream and affect other organs of the body. They influence everything from physical growth to metabolism to sexuality, plus they affect the organism's response to its environment. The hypothalamus secretes corticotropin releasing factor (CRF), which stimulates the pituitary gland to release adrenocorticotropic hormone (ACTH). ACTH causes the adrenal glands, from their unlikely perch atop the kidneys, to release cortisol and epinephrine. Cortisol (a class of hormones called steroids) plus epinephrine are released in response to situations perceived as dangerous (encountering the Big Bad Wolf in the woods) and to prepare the body to "fight or flee." When danger subsides, cortisol and epinephrine levels return to normal. Stress (external: riding a roller coaster; or internal: Am I going to lose my job?) acts as a danger signal and also causes the body to produce higher levels of cortisol and epinephrine. Studies of depressed patients reveal that both corticotropin releasing factor (CRF) and cortisol levels are persistently elevated. This has the effect of keeping the depressed patient in a perpetual state of responding to danger—fighting or fleeing. When depressed patients get well, their production of CRF and cortisol goes down. Knowing this doesn't answer "the chicken or the egg" question. Does a stress response to external or internal danger release cortisol and cause depression, or does depression create a stress response that causes the body to produce more CRF and cortisol? Finally, cortisol alone has an effect on emotions (recall the "'Roid Rage" of the athlete who abuses steroids to increase muscle mass). Interactions between hormones, endocrine glands, and impulses from neurons in the frontal lobe and midbrain are in constant flux, and a variety of complex, finely tuned, feedback mechanisms keep their production at appropriate levels in normal people.

The endocrine system can malfunction and cause disease just like every other organ system in the body. Studying endocrine diseases, just like studying stroke victims, has given us insight into depression. A benign tumor of the pituitary gland (producing excess ACTH) causes the adrenals to make too much cortisol and the result is Cushing's Disease (named after the physician who described it), a disease that, among other things, causes marked changes in mood. Half of these patients have depression, while a little less than a fifth become manic. Why cortisol causes depression in some, mania in others, and no mood change in the third group is not understood. Cortisol and its derivatives are also used as medications for certain diseases (inflammatory and allergic diseases–rheumatoid arthritis and asthma–and in reducing rejection of transplanted organs). These medicines produce side effects in such patients, two of which are depression or mania.

Studies of the interaction of these hormones and chemicals only serve to reinforce the connection between mind and body and establish depression as a systemic disease. Appropriate levels of serotonin in the bloodstream makes platelets less "sticky," and reduces blood clots that are a factor in heart disease and stroke. Depression, with elevated levels of cortisol, makes the body less responsive to insulin, the hormone that processes blood sugar, and thus has an adverse effect on diabetes.

Engineering and Depression

Taking pictures of internal body parts has made great strides since the day when Dr. Roentgen first took a picture of the bones in a hand using X-rays. Positron Emission Tomography (PET scans) has made it possible to take pictures of brain anatomy and has even devised techniques to watch brain parts "work." The pictures can be taken in blue, purple, yellow, and orange colors. In depression, blue and purple colors predominate in certain regions of the brain. Yellow and orange colors predominate when the person is not depressed. The colors have to do with the use of fuel (sugar) in the brain cells (neurons). When more fuel is used, the neurons are more active and produce yellow and orange colors. When less fuel is used, the neurons are less active and produce blue and purple colors.

These techniques reveal that depressed patients have low activity in the frontal lobes and the left prefrontal cortex. (Remember, stroke victims whose left prefrontal cortex is damaged are more likely to be depressed than stroke victims whose right prefrontal cortex is damaged.) When depressed patients recover during medical treatment and/or psychotherapy, the pictures taken by PET scans return to normal and the patterns are the same as those in comparison populations of non-depressed patients.

Epidemiology and Depression

Epidemiology (literally the study of demographics) is the statistical study of populations with various diseases. In depressed populations, epidemiologists attempt to determine what external events might be associated with depression, what symptoms belong in the classification of depression, who is more likely to be affected by depression, and establish if there are social, cultural, familial, or genetic predispositions to depression. Epidemiologists compiled the statistics beginning on page 19 and page 102.

When we assimilate these facts from the sciences about the functioning human organism, we must conclude that the brain (*at a cellular level*) is an organ just like, for instance, the stomach. Our response is to this idea is probably, "Well, of course!" So, when the stomach organ is filled with steak, veggies, and fruit, it churns out chemicals and enzymes that digest and transport them through the wall of the stomach where they are converted to sugar, proteins, and vitamins that nourish the body. Likewise, the brain organ, when stimulated, releases neurotransmitters that flow and recede, and civilization occurs. Our response to that is probably, "Huh?" Because now we understand that the brain is capable of allowing you not only to punch out the bully but also to conceptualize. Anatomy and biochemistry make not only "fight or flight" possible but also art and mathematics, and they allow the organism to adapt and emote.

Civilization flows from this jumble called the brain because a tiny cell called a neuron makes and takes up chemicals and is bathed in hormones. This is both simple and complex and also humbling (and somewhat unnerving, to use a rather humorous word). Molecules released into the gaps between nerve cells make possible devoted love and homicidal anger. Thus, the anatomical, neuropharmacological, genetic, hormonal human being interacts with its environment. Persons, clans, tribes, nations, and populations interact with each other and with a plot of ground, a state, a nation, a continent, and a world with its specific weather, geography, and geology. The result is Attila the Hun, Abraham of Chaldea, Cleopatra, and Richard Speck; also the Norman Conquest, the antebellum South, the Holocaust, and the National Football League; and a bronze sword, the pyramids, the Sistine Chapel, and the Golden Gate Bridge. To say nothing of the Bible, *The Brothers Karamazov, The Jupiter Symphony, Hamlet,* and *Mein Kampf.* Human beings tell stories, sing songs, paint pictures, craft tools, and plant gardens; they also build cities, cathedrals, hospitals, bathtubs, and battleships. And human beings develop depression.

I'm nowhere, Lord,
And I couldn't care less.
It's so still.
Am I on the moon?
Am I on the earth?
Am I here at all?
But, if so, where?
I feel disengaged from life at this moment, Lord.
Time has stopped,
And nothing matters.
I have nowhere to hurry,
No place to go,
No sensible goal.
I might as well be dead.
I want to feel a breeze blow against my face,
Or the hot sun warming me.
I want to feel life, Jesus.
Help me to feel love or anger or laughter.
Help me to care about life again.[2]

Malcolm Boyd, twentieth-century Episcopal priest

---

[2]Malcolm Boyd, *Are You Running with Me, Jesus?* (New York: Discuss Books/Avon, 1968), 28.

The Man Who Couldn't Dance: PART THREE

That night, after dinner, Ernest told Mary, "I lost a good friend today." He related the encounter with Tom, omitting the "company ink" crack.

"What are you going to do?"

"I don't know."

Mary was reluctant to offer advice. Over several years, she had taken different approaches to Ernest's moods. She had pointed out his successes: education, career, children, financial security, community service, military record.

"Don't patronize me."

She had suggested a different church.

"Church doesn't make any difference."

"Then stop going."

"I can't."

She had suggested a long vacation, changing jobs, or moving to a different town.

"I'm not a gypsy."

She had suggested marriage counseling or support groups.

"I hate weepy, touchy-feely stuff."

She had suggested that he see his doctor. Talk to a psychiatrist.

"I'm not gonna puke my guts up to some shrink! I'm not Woody-the-therapy-junky-Allen"...

CHAPTER THREE

Treating the Physical Disease

Look, O LORD, and see
how worthless I have become.
Is it nothing to you, all you who pass by?
Look and see
if there is any sorrow like my sorrow.

LAMENTATIONS 1:11b–12a

In Western culture, the term *medicine* has been associated almost exclusively with therapies rooted in the natural sciences and the scientific method. Such therapeutic methods may be grouped under the headings of pharmacology, physical modalities, and psychotherapy. There are, however, cultures throughout the world that approach disease and healing with different concepts and methodology. For purposes of this book, we have coined the term *Complementary and Alternative Therapies* (CAT) for these combinations of therapy. These therapies range from Eastern traditions thousands of years old (acupuncture) to new-age remedies (crystals). The methods may be grouped broadly under two headings: alternative care and general health improvement.

Pharmacological Therapy (Medicine)

Science currently understands healthy function of the brain at the cellular level (the neuron) as follows:

■ Neurons produce neurotransmitters (serotonin, norepinephrine, and dopamine) and release them from its axon into the gap between it and other neurons.

■ Neurotransmitters flow across the gap and bind to receptor sites of the receiving neuron and "tell it" to perform its function.

■ After the neuron receives the message, it releases the neuro-transmitter back into the gap.

■ The neuron that released the neurotransmitter in the first place takes it back (reuptake), or enzymes destroy any extra neurotransmitters remaining in the gap.

■ Neurotransmitters are at the basis of normal cellular function and are found not only in the brain but also throughout the body. Depression is a systemic disease.

Medication is usually the first choice in the treatment of depression. Drugs that treat depression are called antidepressants. All of them work by increasing the amount of neurotransmitters (serotonin, norepinephrine, and dopamine) available to keep the messages moving between neurons. They do this in two ways. One is to prevent the neurotransmitters from being taken back into the axon of the neuron (blocking the reuptake of the neurotransmitter). These drugs are called reuptake inhibitors. The second method is to block the enzyme that breaks down the neurotransmitters. Since this enzyme is monoamine oxidase, these drugs are called monoamine oxidase inhibitors.

Classes of Antidepressants

Selective Serotonin Reuptake Inhibitors (SSRIs)

This class of drugs blocks the reuptake of serotonin back into the neuron. If more serotonin is left in the gap between nerve cells, more (or more effective) messages are communicated between neurons. There are some side effects of SSRIs, including drowsiness, sleep disturbances, headache, jitteriness, and tremors. Up to one-third of people taking SSRIs have reduced interest in sex and delayed or absent orgasms. Prozac is the classic, and first, selective serotonin reuptake inhibitor. It was released in 1988 and is so well known that it is now part of the language of our culture. It was followed by Zoloft, Paxil, Luvox, and Celexa. The effect on depression does not seem to be related to the amount taken, so small doses have a beneficial effect. This widens the margin of safety if taken in an accidental or intentional overdose.

Monoamine Oxidase Inhibitors (MAOIs)

Monoamine oxidase inhibitors were initially developed to treat tuberculosis (TB)—a bacterial infection that no longer holds the terror that it once did, because modern science has largely defeated it. When this initial anti-tuberculous drug, Iproniazid, was given to tuberculosis patients, it was noted that their mood often improved (more than could be accounted for because they were getting well from TB). Serendipity stepped in and prompted research on this phenomenon. It was discovered that Iproniazid inactivated an enzyme (monoamine oxidase) that broke down serotonin and norepinephrine. Increased amounts of these neurotransmitters improved the message delivery system between neurons and relieved depression. Again, side effects include jitteriness, sleep disturbances, dizziness, nausea, and sexual dysfunction. Monoamine oxidase is also present in the intestine and liver and MAOIs can interfere with metabolism of certain foods (red wines, beer, beans, and certain cheeses), causing dangerous increases in blood pressure. MAOIs are less frequently prescribed because of this drawback. Nardil, Marplan, and Parnate are trade names of MAOIs.

Tricyclic Antidepressants (TCAs)

This class of drugs (called tricyclics because they are made up of three-ringed compounds linked together) block reuptake of both serotonin and norepinephrine, leaving more of these chemicals free to transmit their messages. Common side effects of the tricyclics are sedation, constipation, urinary retention, dry mouth, and blurred vision. Side effects that are more serious are changes in heart rate or rhythm and a drop in blood pressure, especially when a person abruptly stands or sits up. The benefits of TCAs are related to the dosage, so higher dosages may help depression more but that nudges the patient closer to side effects. The first tricyclic was Thorazine, a medication developed to treat seizure disorders (serendipity). More recent TCAs include Sinequan, Elavil, Ludiomil, and Tofranil. Tricyclics are less frequently prescribed because they can be fatal if taken in an overdose.

Serotonin Antagonist Reuptake Inhibitors (SARIs)

This class of drugs not only reduce the reuptake of serotonin by the neuron that released it but also block specific serotonin receptors sites on the receiving neuron. The net result is a greater quantity of serotonin to deliver messages between nerve cells. Side effects include nausea, sedation, jitteriness, blurred vision, constipation, and a drop in blood pressure when suddenly standing or sitting up. Serzone and Desyrel are trade names for SARIs. Serzone reportedly produces less sexual dysfunction than SSRIs and MAOIs.

Norepinephrine Reuptake Inhibitors (NRIs)

These drugs selectively inhibit the reuptake of norepinephrine so more of this neurotransmitter is present at the synapse of neurons. They may also inhibit reuptake of the neurotransmitter dopamine. Side effects include headache, dry mouth, sleep disturbances, nausea, and constipation. Wellbutrin is a well-known NRI.

Drugs with Mixed Effects

Effexor is in a different class than SSRIs and TCAs, but it has a similar effect on depression. It reduces the reuptake of serotonin at low doses (like SSRIs) and blocks the reuptake of norepinephrine at higher dosages (like TCAs). The side effects are similar to both SSRIs and TCAs, but Effexor also can cause elevated blood pressure (like MAOIs).

Benzodiazepines

Benzodiazepines block dopamine (a third neurotransmitter) receptor sites on neurons. They have been used since the 1970s as sedatives, tranquilizers, muscle relaxants, anticonvulsants, and to reduce anxiety. More recently, they have been used in the treatment of manic-depression. Librium, Xanax, Valium, Tranxene, Restoril, Klonapin, and Ativan are benzodiazepines. Side effects include sedation, dry mouth, constipation, drop in blood pressure on standing or sitting up, weight gain, and sexual dysfunction. They may affect muscle tone and movement (Parkinson-like symptoms) and cause restlessness. It is possible to become addicted to benzodiazepines and this is made worse with alcohol. These drugs are usually prescribed for shorter periods of time.

Lithium, Tegretol, and Depakote

Lithium is a naturally occurring element (the third element in the periodic table) sold under several trade names (Lithobid, Lithotabs, Eskalith) and is unsurpassed in treating manic-depression. Its mechanism of action is unknown, but it stabilizes mood and helps prevent swings between depression and mania. Manic-depressive patients on Lithium have nine times fewer suicides than patients not taking this drug. Tegretol and Depakote have anticonvulsant properties (reduce seizures) and neuropharmacologists speculate that somehow this property helps manic-depression. Lithium, Tegretol, and Depakote reduce the frequency and severity of manic attacks, and the first two reduce depression as well. Side effects of these drugs include sedation, nausea, weight gain, loss of balance, skin rash, impaired liver function, and lowered white blood count.

There is no perfect antidepressant medication. No single medication works in every patient and all have side effects. The physician chooses one and uses it for a sufficient period of time to judge its effectiveness. About one third of patients don't do well with the first drug they try and must take another. Usually, the SSRIs are the first choice to treat depression. Lithium is the drug of choice in treating manic-depression. About one third of depressed patients take antidepressants for a period of time (many months at the very least) to "jump-start" their depressed brains and then are able to discontinue the medication. Another third will have other episodes of depression and need to take antidepressants again. The final third seem to slide into depression each time they stop their medication and need to take it permanently.

Patients have many reservations about taking antidepressants. Some reservations are psychological: "Taking medicines means I'm weak…" "If I take drugs, I'm admitting I'm sick…" Some reservations are spiritual: "Taking a pill means I don't have enough faith…" Some are psychosocial: "I don't like to put foreign substances in my body…" (In this age when more and more chemicals are released into our environment—arsenic, mercury, lead—and we have been Erin Brockovitched, such fears are understandable.) Some reservations to taking medication are physical: "I'm afraid I'll become addicted…" This is a realistic concern with some medicines. Good doctors weigh benefits and risks when prescribing any drug, and inform their patients about side effects. Good doctors monitor their patients for the appearance of side effects. When a doctor says a particular medication will help you and educates you about the risks, discuss it and make an informed decision, but don't refuse to take it just because there might be side effects. After all, every medication has benefits (therapy) and risks (side effects). The package insert on aspirin (a drug so safe it is sold without prescription and several tons of it are taken in America every year) lists ulcers and dangerous bleeding as side effects.

Physical Therapy

Electroconvulsive Therapy

Electroconvulsive therapy (previously called electroshock therapy) is one of the oldest and most effective treatments for severe and incapacitating depression. It has a lurid reputation because it is associated with the worst days of mental hospitals as places of horror. The therapy is also tainted in popular culture by *One Flew over the Cuckoo's Nest,* in which Jack Nicholson wisecracked, "A little dab'll do ya," as they smeared grease on his temples and applied the electrodes that sent him into a muscle-wracking convulsion. This therapy fell into disuse when antidepressants first became available because it was hoped they would provide a miracle cure. However, with the realization that one third of depressed patients don't respond to any medications, the use of ECT has increased in the past twenty years. Consequently, ECT is being further refined. Seizures and fractures associated with brittle bones (osteoporosis) have been reduced by administration of general anesthesia. (Of course, there is some risk to general anesthesia itself.) Also, classical right- and left-sided ECT interfered with certain memory and learning functions (cognitive thinking), even though this generally appears to reverse itself after several months. Modifications in ECT equipment now make it possible to deliver electrical current only to the right side of the brain. This has proved to be just as effective in reducing depression, and appears to interfere less with memory and cognitive thought.

Electroshock therapy is usually given three times a week for up to eight to twelve treatments. It is often, but not always, administered while the depressed patient is hospitalized. It may be administered as an outpatient, but still within an outpatient facility that can safely provide anesthesia and recovery care. This therapy usually alleviates depression more quickly than medication (one month of therapy as compared to several months or more), but the depression tends to recur in a few months, especially if ECT is stopped abruptly. It is standard practice to gradually reduce ECT, either by lengthening the period of time between the last treatments or by beginning concurrent antidepressant and/or lithium therapy to prevent relapse. The combined use of ECT in the short term and medication for the long term is an effective treatment for depression.

Light Therapy

Seasonal Affective Disorder (SAD–an acronym too clever by half) is characterized by depression at seasons of the year with less sunshine and shorter days. The depression can be mild or severe and can even include suicidal thoughts. Exposing these patients to banks of lights helps lift their depression. This low-cost, low-tech, simple process is a useful tool but patients have to be exposed for at least an hour each day. The SSRI antidepressants also help SAD patients.

Repeated Transcranial Magnetic Stimulation (RTMS)

Applying magnets to the right side of the brain (RTMS) produces a weak, localized magnetic field that helps alleviate depression. The patient experiences no discomfort and the procedure doesn't require general anesthesia or sedation. There seems to be little interference with memory. A strong magnetic field applied to the brain will induce a convulsion (as does ECT). Convulsive TMS is experimental and not yet as effective in treating depression as ECT, but researchers hope that convulsions produced by magnetic fields will have a beneficial effect on depression without some of the side effects of ECT (memory loss and disturbance in cognitive thinking).

Vagus Nerve Stimulation

The vagus nerves connect to parts of the brain that are involved in depression (frontal lobes and left prefrontal cortex, thalamus, hypothalamus, and amygdala). The vagus nerves leave the brain, pass down either side of the neck, and connect to other body organs (heart, blood vessels, stomach, sweat glands). Stimulation of the vagus nerves increases the level of neurotransmitters such as serotonin. With this experimental treatment for depression, a small electrical device is implanted under the skin on the left chest (much like a cardiac pacemaker) and connected to the left vagus nerve in the neck. The device is programmed to send a small electrical current to the vagus nerve for thirty seconds every five minutes day and night. The patient is unaware of the device and the vagal stimulation, but it helps alleviate depression in some people.

Gene Therapy

An exciting possibility for therapy of genetically influenced disease is the manipulation of genes to "cure" the disease. Science is currently genetically engineering corn and other plants and this has raised alarms about the safety of eating such foods. Imagine the impact of genetically engineering a human being to eliminate depression. Profound discussions in the fields of law and bioethics, disciplines that were unknown a few decades ago, will precede any such therapy.

Psychotherapy

It has long been known that talking out your troubles can be good for you. At the very least, telling your story to a sympathetic listener assures you that you are not alone when you are desolate. Since the nineteenth century, this type of treatment has been termed psychotherapy. Psychotherapy works on the cerebral cortex where learning, concentration, rational thought, planning, and problem solving reside. Psychotherapy can teach patients to handle situations of interpersonal conflict. It can support and sustain them through trying and perilous times. It can encourage them to keep appointments with various therapists and to take their medication. It can place them in touch with support groups and programs to treat substance abuse.

It can take the lead in coordinating collaborative therapeutic efforts. It can serve as a bridge during dangerous times between hospital discharge and continued recovery. It can support family members and friends and involve them in productive methods of therapy. It can inquire about suicidal thoughts and plans and see that potentially lethal means of suicide (guns, ropes, alcohol, knives, razors, poisons) are removed from their homes or places of business.

This broad field merits a thorough discussion and we refer you to chapter 5.

Complementary and Alternative Therapies (CAT)

Therapies under the CAT umbrella include, but are not limited to, acupuncture, yoga, biofeedback, meditation, relaxation techniques, aromatherapy, massage, herbal treatments, tai chi, homeopathy, naturopathy, and dance therapy. Other treatment concepts appear at regular intervals, and all have been used to treat depression. There is little doubt that many of these treatments make a person feel better and they are safe.

It is unarguable that surrounding a person with pleasant scents improves mood, at least temporarily. Keeping pets, if one is so inclined, is good for people. It gives them companionship and something to care for. The beneficial effects of touch are well documented. Babies "fail to thrive" when placed in settings where they are not touched. Studies have shown that many of the elderly, especially those who live alone, go to doctors simply to be touched in a safe, appropriate manner, and that alone improves their well-being. Yoga appears to reduce stress and to improve physical conditioning and flexibility. Concentrated "breath work" is an integral part of yoga (but it can also be practiced by itself), and it appears to improve depression, anxiety, and panic attacks. Traditional Chinese medicine posits that good health depends on the life force (*qi* [pronounced "chee"]) flowing harmoniously among the elements of wood, fire, earth, metal, and water; the pathogenic factors of cold, wind, dryness, heat, dampness, and fire; and the emotions of joy, anger, anxiety, obsession, sadness, horror, and fear. This kind of language appeals to certain temperaments because the language is profound but unfathomable, cites concrete elements and emotions, and has the force of a mystical religion.

Western medicine begins with the bias that anything not proven by the scientific method is speculative. We know that therapy sometimes works just because people believe it will (the power of suggestion—mind over matter). In every double-blind study using drugs and placebos, a percentage of patients on the placebo get better.

Success in treating diseases with herbal remedies is often measured by testimonials and success stories (anecdotal evidence). Sound research to identify the active ingredient, establish correct dosage, and monitor for side effects has generally not been done. It's important to note that CAT is big business (as is Western medicine) and it's almost impossible to change an industry (think automobile). Medical doctors have been surprised by studies that found that consumers spend almost as much annually on CAT as they do Western medicine (without the benefit of insurance), and that more patients seek out CAT therapists than visit medical doctors.

There are at least five reasons people seek complementary and alternative medicine:

■ Medical doctors sometimes seem more interested in laboratory tests and technical procedures than the patient.

■ Western medicine has extended the normal life span, but longer life is not synonymous with wholeness and health.

■ Western medical science has been unable to successfully treat many chronic and recurrent diseases.

■ Patients will go to almost any length to find relief from their disease.

■ Their treatment of choice makes them feel better.

On the other hand, Western medical science has several reservations about complementary and alternative therapies:

■ Complementary and Alternative Therapies generally aren't undergirded by a unified theory, nor are they coordinated in any manner.

■ Effectiveness and safety of CAT therapies are not usually evaluated for objective, reproducible, proven results. Very few herbs have been subjected to controlled, random, double-blind studies (neither the patient nor the researcher knows who is receiving the drug or the placebo). This is just now being done in various centers, but clinical trials take time.

■ These therapies usually aren't integrated in any manner and the patient remains alone through the course of treatment. Solitary treatment is not ideal therapy for depression.

Patients have choices in therapy and they are exercising that right, but common sense is required to avoid falling for every trendy cure *de jour*. Patients should be knowledgeable about alternative choices and use good judgment. They should be familiar with the risks. Guard against extravagant claims, especially testimonials. Remember, herbs and supplements are not regulated by the Food and Drug Administration, consequently purity and dosage may vary in the manufacturing process. Herbs that have pharmacological activity have side effects, cause allergic reactions, and are toxic, as are prescription medications. Ginkgo biloba has anticoagulant properties that may cause bleeding (strokes, bowel hemorrhage, or excessive bleeding during surgery). Soy contains natural estrogens and there is concern it might have adverse effects in women with potential for breast or uterine cancer. The active ingredient in *ma huang* is ephedrine and it can cause dangerous elevations in blood pressure. Saint John's wort has some effect on serotonin, norepinephrine, and dopamine— molecules implicated in depression—but controlled studies have failed to document actual clinical improvement in depression. The new rage for treating depression, liver disease, and osteoarthritis is SAMe (S-adenosylmethionine). It appears to boost dopamine and serotonin activity, but it is not clear how clinically useful it is in depression. When used in manic-depression, SAMe may cause mania. When patients visit medical doctors, they sometimes don't tell their physician what herbs and supplements they are taking, either because they don't think of them as "medicines" or because they are embarrassed to admit they have sought alternative therapies. Tell your doctor everything you take and do to improve your health.

People should guard against unscrupulous practitioners in any area of medicine. Regard all therapeutic claims with a healthy skepticism. Remember P.T. Barnum's aphorism, "It's a sin not to take a sucker's money." Having said all of this, a new kind of medicine may be emerging called integrative medicine. In this context, all healers would work together, drawing on each discipline's individual strengths. The key word is discipline, indicating that the approach to a medical theory and treatment is disciplined. Think clearly, reflect honestly, and integrate wisely.

Overall Health Improvement

In treating depression, as in treating other illnesses, the patient should address all of the aspects of a healthy lifestyle that contribute to being well. First, practice good nutrition. Medical science has known for almost three centuries that certain nutrients are vital in preventing specific diseases. (Vitamin C deficiency produces a disease called scurvy; vitamin D deficiency produces a disease called rickets.) However, for the past seventy-five years, medicine has been entranced by the tricks it could perform, and prodigious feats they were—repair of birth defects, open-heart surgery, brain surgery, organ transplants, cancer therapy, endoscopy, and replacement body parts! Neglected studies in nutrition are just now catching up with advances in techniques. We are slowly unraveling the hitherto mysterious interplay of many nutrients in our food supply. Antioxidants (such as Vitamins E and A and beta-carotene), free radicals, SAMe, folic acid, omega-3 fatty acids, and coenzyme Q10 promote heart health, brain health, and may improve depression, while cholesterol adversely affects the heart and circulatory system. Diets should be low in saturated fats and trans-fats, and contain generous proportions of fruits, vegetables, whole grains, fish, nuts, and flaxseed oil—just like your mother told you! Boring, right? It's easier to take a supplement. Interestingly, there is no good evidence that taking vitamins and supplements in pill form works as well as when they are consumed in natural foods. Beyond the pure science of nutrition, good food in good company is a healing experience of body, mind, and spirit that can best be described under the heading of table fellowship.

Second, avoid negative health influences of smoking and substance abuse. Caffeine (chocolate, tea, coffee), when taken in large amounts and close to bedtime, causes disturbed sleep patterns. Alcohol, as a sedative, is a depressant. It may make a depressed person feel better temporarily, but it interferes with thinking, judgment, and sleep. It reduces inhibitions, contributes to antisocial behavior, and reduces the effectiveness of antidepressant medication.

Third, exercise regularly. *Any* type of exercise releases endorphins that boost neurotransmitters and helps alleviate depression. Choose an enjoyable and communal activity such as dance, jazzercise, or a team sport. Exercising with others lends social support and enhances mood elevation. Take walks; alone is certainly fine, but the company of a friend or relative adds mutuality. Participation in such activities, of course, assumes that the depressed person's disease is not so severe they are unable to get out of bed.

Finally, the restorative power of sleep, though not fully understood, has been known since antiquity. Again, Mom was right. Get a good night's sleep. We neglect these simple steps to good health at our peril.

It remains to be said that good health is not perfect health. Alleviating depression does not create the perfect mood, but there is hope for depressed people, their families, friends, and coworkers. There are so many modalities of therapy to improve depression that all the rigors of this disease need not be suffered. Recognize depression! Get help!

O God,
My words are heavy and dull.
They do not fly heavenward,
But lie in my gut,
Leaden,
Listless,
Refusing to rise.
I speak to you out of sheer habit,
Not conviction,
Prying loose the language of prayer
That will not spring to my aid.
O God,
I have no joy;
No gladness to draw me into the bliss of your love.
O God,
I have no tears.
No burden of sorrow that throws my soul into your
    compassionate embrace.
O God,
I have no anger.
No rage with which to stir you to justice.
No fury with which to rouse your terrible mercy.
I am empty.
I am mute.
I am a wasteland.
I am lost.
And so are you.
What shall we do, old friend, to find each other and ourselves
    once again?
If there is any grace,
If there is any mercy,
If there is any hope,
May it once more pass between us.[1]

Charisa L. Hunter-Crump,
Contemporary Pastor, Disciples of Christ

---

[1]Unpublished writings of Charisa L. Hunter-Crump.

The Man Who Couldn't Dance: PART FOUR

Mary knocked lightly on the door before she entered Ernest's study. He sat behind his desk, backlit by the fading light of a dying day, turning a cigarette lighter in his hands. The face of the chrome lighter was embossed with metal facsimiles of a Ranger tab and the First Air Cav shoulder patch. He opened the cover. The wick had never been lit.

"Are you okay?" Mary asked.

"Yeah." Ernest snapped the cover closed and placed the lighter back on his desk, carefully balancing it so it stood on end, the symbols of his service unit facing him. It struck him that the lighter resembled a domino. He used to think that countries stood on end. Like dominos.

"Do you wish you'd stayed in the army?"

Ernest snorted. "God, no!"

"I thought maybe you missed it."

"No." Ernest frowned and shook his head. "But I miss the clarity."

"Let's go out tonight." A desperate plea. A yearning to break the cycle of negativism. Mary ached with the fear that Ernie's problems were all about her. She had failed him. "How about a movie?"

"Not in the mood."

"Take me dancing."

"I'm just too tired."

"You used to love to dance." Mary did a few steps and held out her arms in invitation.

Earnest shook his head wearily.

Mary's voice broke. "I'm lonely, Ernie."

Ernest reached deep inside himself for a response. The place where his feelings had been was a wasteland. Scorched and barren. He wanted to respond, but he couldn't. "I'm going to bed."

Mary called after him. "Maybe this weekend I'll go see my folks." She added hopefully, "Unless you'd like to do something."

"No, I think the visit would be good for you."

Ernest lay awake for long hours. His emotional scale ranged from disgust to rage to fear. He knew he was slowly cutting himself off from everything and everyone. How could he behave so wretchedly to Mary? The energy required to simply step into her arms when she asked to go dancing was more than he could muster. The distance between them seemed measured in light years, not dance steps. And poor Tom. Tom had avoided him at the office for a week. It would be tough to make things right with him. If he had learned anything, it was that he couldn't talk his way out of something he'd behaved himself into. And Tom was right about the company ink. He'd had a shooting-star affair. For a while, he felt good. He was alive. He couldn't sustain the relationship and was soon involved with someone else. More tawdry. No excuses this time about true love. Fornication released a burst of passion that elevated his mood. A series of affairs followed. Then he no longer had the energy for women. It wasn't the adultery. It was the lying. The continual deceit with Mary was too corrosive. More self-hate. Frenzied activities replaced sexual indiscretions. Travel. It seemed he'd been everywhere twice and done everything ten times. Nothing measured up to his expectations. He had even returned to Vietnam to face down the ghosts. There was no resolution, reconciliation, or restitution. He tried all the toys. Golf, tennis, skiing, boats. Too much liquor. A DUI expunged from his record with prestige, power, and money. He bought a Harley. Death wish? Tom derisively called him a RUB—a rich, urban biker. *Rub-a-dub-dub. Three men in a tub. Aye, there's the rub. Rub me the wrong way. I'll rub you out.* Ernest dozed. He felt Mary slip into bed. She rolled against him, placing a hand on his chest as she slid a thigh up across his pelvis in invitation. He turned away. Regret and remorse flayed him. He finally fell asleep, only to awaken a few hours later. The ruminations rippled through his consciousness as he stared at the beamed ceiling. *Rub-a-dub-dub...*

CHAPTER FOUR

The Social Disease

Be gracious to me, O LORD, for I am in distress;
my eye wastes away from grief,
my soul and body also.
For my life is spent with sorrow,
and my years with sighing;
my strength fails because of my misery,
and my bones waste away.
I am the scorn of all my adversaries,
a horror to my neighbors,
an object of dread to my acquaintances;
those who see me in the street flee from me.

PSALM 31:9–11

Depression is a social disease. When the "self" is sick, there is no place to hide and no way of escape. Every relationship depressed persons have is tainted. They can, as the psalmist says, become a horror to their neighbors and an object of dread to their friends. Far worse, they can become a contagious presence within their families, spreading gloom, dissatisfaction, fear, uncertainty, doubt, grief, anger, and anxiety. The disease begins to cast a pall over everything they touch. The awareness of what they are doing coupled with the inability to stop it feeds the depression and fills them with loathing. Being around a depressed person is emotionally draining. It breeds depression in others. Whether we are depressed or live with someone who is depressed, it's important to look at the dynamics of this social disease as it affects and undermines various relationships.

The Depleted Spouse

There is always a debate about whether depression causes troubled marriages or troubled marriages cause depression. The answer is probably both. It can be a vicious circle. There is no doubt that depression in one spouse puts enormous stress on the other spouse. When a family member develops cancer or heart disease, it's not very long before the others know something is wrong and seek help. The onset of depression is often insidious and stealthily overtakes the afflicted spouse. The other spouse soldiers on in grim determination, bewildered by the poisonous atmosphere that has taken up residence in the marriage. The spouse may begin to doubt or blame himself or herself for all the trouble. What's wrong with me? If only I were better, sexier, more attentive, smarter, made more money, didn't spend so much money. Is my spouse having an affair? Is my spouse considering divorce? Is my spouse taking drugs? What can I do to fix this mess?

Once the depression is recognized, there may be an initial rallying of support to deal with the sadness, anger, withdrawal, and irritability. Excuses are made for the depressed spouse's behavior and moodiness. The healthy spouse patiently endures in the hope that the mood will pass, but when the depression is chronic and unrelieved, the healthy spouse will become depleted. Energy and patience fail. There are no more excuses. The foundations of the relationship become eroded. Intimacy disappears, needs won't be met, and hope evaporates. The entire fabric of the marriage unravels and it may be difficult or impossible to repair. Studies have shown that depression causes more family dysfunction than most other illnesses. Only terminal cancer affects families as much as depression, and in the case of cancer it usually brings families together rather than driving them apart.

The Parent/Child Gridlock

When a parent is depressed, it inevitably affects the children. Distance, anger, and negativity corrode the child's self-esteem and sense of security. Children are quick to accept blame for dysfunction, arguments, and bad moods. Communication is blocked, along with the flow of emotional support and affection. Stress and anxiety pollute the family environment. Children begin to feel they must "walk on eggshells," becoming hypersensitive to every situation and fearful of receiving the brunt of anger and criticism. Children may begin to act out in other social settings (school, neighborhood, activities). Some studies show that depression has more negative effects on child development than psychotic disorders. The depressed parent and the vulnerable child may become locked in an emotional traffic jam.

When a child is depressed, it will also affect the family. Depression in children and adolescents is often hard to recognize because they are going through physical and emotional changes that normally affect mood and behavior. Children, in particular, may not exhibit classic symptoms of adult depression. Their depression is often expressed as anger, not sadness. In teenagers, too, depression is often evidenced by irritability and anger. Besides, everyone knows that teenagers are simply too weird, right? Is my kid sullen or sick, calloused or crazy, stupid or sad, moody or mad? Symptoms of teenage depression may simply be passed over as a "phase," but recognition and treatment is critical. Consequently, when evaluating their children's mental health, parents first need to take into account a family history of depression. A positive family history for depression makes it statistically more likely that a child will suffer from depressive illness. Further, parents must pay attention to their children and teenagers and be aware of subtle, persistent changes in appearance, behavior, and mood. Take note if there is more than ordinary weight gain or loss. Be alert to persistent, unremitting negativity and irritability. Observe sleep habits, particularly if a teenager is unable to get out of bed in the morning. Inability to get out of bed may be a classic sign of depression, but perhaps they have a sleep disorder. Are they going to bed at 10 p.m. and lying awake till 3 a.m.? Parents must also remember there are many things they don't know about their children after they begin school and as they attain the independence of adolescence. Perhaps they are being bullied at school. Maybe they are developing an eating disorder. Are there signs of bingeing, purging, or anorexia? Sudden changes in behavior may indicate they are abusing alcohol or drugs. Perhaps they have become sexually active, creating stress and uncertainty. Fear of pregnancy will affect mood and behavior.

Parents must keep lines of communication open with their children. It must begin early. The phrase, "use it or lose it," has never been truer. Established early, it's easier to converse with your teenagers. Return to the "ancient" habit of having meals together because it creates the possibility for conversation in an atmosphere of pleasure and nourishment. Ask questions. If answers are forthcoming, listen! You are not looking so much for information as for insight. Listen without interrupting, offering immediate advice, pronouncing judgment, or being critical. A good response may be, "I don't understand that. Can you tell me more about it?" Unfortunately, communication with children is often one of the first things in the parent-child relationship to fail. By the time serious concerns manifest themselves, the communication gap is almost unbridgeable.

Fractured Friendships

Friendships also suffer from the presence of depression. We hurt most those who care most about us. Friendships are difficult to maintain when they are marred by free-floating anger, hypersensitivity, withdrawal, and bad moods. Friends on the receiving end of such frustrating behavior begin to feel like emotional punching bags. They don't know how to react and feel a deep sense of loss. Free and easy discourse becomes tentative and anxious. It's difficult to recognize that their friend's behavior is caused by depression, and they begin to doubt their worth as a friend. The sense of mutuality in the relationship withers, and the friendship is no longer worth the trouble.

The Fouled Workplace

Unfortunately, offices, industries, businesses, hospitals, educational institutions, corporations, factories, and churches have their fair share of dysfunction as manifested by cliques, maneuvering, game-playing, paper shuffling, pettiness, incompetence, blame shifting, indifference, and even meanness. Also, unfortunately, the healthiest of us contribute to it. Under normal circumstances, most people are able to deal with this general foolishness and carry on. Not so in depression. A depressed person is marginally functional and has no reserves for coping with office politics. Work suffers, but the person also contributes significantly to fouling the workplace. Depression not only robs sufferers from joy in their vocation but also may cost them their job simply because their disease won't be tolerated. Bosses, supervisors, and key coworkers should be informed about the diagnosis of depression and integrated into therapy as part of the support system.

Social Intervention

Everyone has times of disappointment, unhappiness, grief, fatigue, and loss. Everyone has been down. Everyone has been ready to give up. However, these times do not last and are not clinical depression. Depression progresses slowly and inexorably to a fixed mental and physical state that lasts months and years. Sometimes persons recognize that they are having the symptoms of depression and set about to overcome it. They try to "buck up" or "knuckle down." They think positively. They exert more willpower. They pray more fervently and seek a deeper faith. Sometimes they change jobs, spouses, churches, or geography to cure their mood. They may go on spending sprees, begin sexual liaisons, or throw themselves into some activity to lift their spirits. Such things may even help for a while, in spite of the upheaval in their lives.

They may seek relief in drugs or alcohol. Sometimes the drugs are recreational and illegal; sometimes they are prescription medications. It isn't that difficult to persuade a doctor to provide sleeping pills or "nerve" medicine. Doctors are programmed to be sympathetic and help people in distress. That is their calling. Such medicine might temporarily promote sleep or relieve stress, but neither are good medications for depression and they are addictive. The depressed person may also turn to alcohol in an attempt to self-medicate. Alcohol may also provide temporary relief from stress and promote a sense of ease, but this too is an illusory, short-lived, and false solution. It is also dangerous. The combination of alcohol and depression are factors in suicide. Even more destructive are alcohol and drugs (legal or recreational). The mix is explosive and lethal.

At other times, people slip slowly into a deep depression without recognizing it. They have neither the insight nor the energy to embark on self-help or self-starter regimens. Depressed persons often attempt to isolate themselves, their own sense of worthlessness leading them to believe no one will want to be with them. Loneliness itself deepens the depression. Under a different set of circumstances, persons may refuse to accept that they suffer from depression. They think they are too strong, too educated, too bright, or too blessed to be depressed. They see no reason for their depression so they deny it. When confronted with the possibility by a family member, friend, coworker, or health professional, they reject the idea and sometimes express displeasure or anger.

There are a number of reasons for these different reactions. Chief among them is that when the very "self" is sick, the perception of self is distorted. Depression prevents clear thinking. Chemical changes in the brain can't be seen or felt in the course of daily existence. Genetic factors don't manifest themselves from moment to moment in self-awareness. There is also the embarrassment and stigma associated with having a mental disease. In ancient times, mental illness carried the stigma of demon possession. In modern times, it carries the stigma of character flaws, moral failure, and spiritual weakness. Some people worry about the shame and social disapproval that often accompanies a diagnosis of depression. Others simply refuse to address the issue out of fear and ignorance. Families sometimes collude in denying depression for fear of the same stigmas or social disapprovals. When families ignore or deny the presence of depression in a family member and fail to seek treatment, they allow or enable the depression to deepen. An unspoken, carefully avoided, dreadful family secret saps the life out of the family. When "something" is clearly going on, but that "something" is either not known or not acknowledged, a secure family life is undermined. Facing up to problems and addressing them is evidence of honesty and courage and opens up the family to the possibility of help.

Family members and others close to depressed people must intervene. Depressed people must not be allowed to deny their illness, persist in the delusion that they can deal with the symptoms out of their own resources, or close themselves off from the support and companionship of their families. Intervention must be done with full knowledge of the difficulties. It will probably generate anger and hostility.

When intervention occurs, everyone in the family has some role in treatment and should become involved in the therapy. This does not mean that all members of the family will see a therapist, though it may. It does mean that all members of the family need to be informed about what is going on, appropriate to their age and ability to understand. This affirms that everyone is a significant part of the life of the family and establishes that the family is indivisible. Everyone should be educated about the disease, its treatment, and its prognosis. Every member of the family must be protected from being sucked into the vortex of depression. Children must be assured that they are not to blame for a parent's illness. Parents must know that they are not to blame for a child's disease.

Adequate, reasoned, well-directed support by the family promotes recovery in the depressed family member and reduces collateral damage to the family. Get help from all the resources available to you—medical, psychological, social, and spiritual. Without help, the downward spiral of illness, unhappiness, recrimination, anger, and guilt is disastrous. Properly attended to, addressing depression within the family can bring a new and deepened sense of family worth and cohesion.

Finally, if you are the depressed member of the family, it's important for you to accept the insight and intervention of those closest to you. When depressed, it's difficult to recognize and monitor our own moods. We must listen to others—family, friends, coworkers, and health care professionals. Intervention is not criticism. Encouragement to get help is not disparagement. Treatment is not shameful. Therapy is not weakness. These are the first steps to hope in a new and renewed future.

O God,
We know that you are with us
From our beginning to our end,
Our birth to our dying.

We know that you are with us
In the midst of every birth and death,
Whether physical, or spiritual, or emotional,
That beats out the rhythm of our days and years.
At times, your presence is overwhelmingly tangible,
At other times mysterious and shadowed.
But sometimes it is your absence
That is tangible and we doubt you altogether.
Or we treat you with contempt
Because you seem so impotent,
So irrelevant,
So aloof.
Turn, O Lord! How long?
Have compassion on your servant.
The rhythm of the world's life
And the rhythm of our own lives
Come together in a surreal dance of syncopation and echo.
We hear a rumor of suicide,
Watch the murder of random victims,
Listen to plans of war,
See images of chaos in streets of rubble,
Eavesdrop on brutality,
Catch hideous glimpses of hunger and hatred.
And we press our bodies to the world's pain
And spin a dangerous dance of
Anger, depression, loathing, and dread.
But you are life, how can we doubt you?
You are life, how can we scorn you?
Teach us a different rhythm.
Lead us in a new dance.
One of light and hope and passion and healing.
Show us how to take as our partner the life of the world,
To press the world's body close to ours,
And gently, step by step and beat by beat,
Move forward, and outward, and inward with joy.[1]

Charisa L. Hunter-Crump
Contemporary Pastor, Disciples of Christ

---

[1]Unpublished writings of Charisa L. Hunter-Crump.

The Man Who Couldn't Dance: PART FIVE

Mary probed gently about Ernest's visit to the psychiatrist. He recognized her anxiety. Knew he was the source. More guilt. Their relationship used to be one of easy conversation and camaraderie. Now she tiptoed around the edges of his life. Venturing into it with trepidation. Afraid the wrong question, the unsolicited bit of advice, the slightest criticism might set off one of his downward spirals into the dark pit where nothing lived but recrimination, regret, negativity, and hostility.

It was hard for Ernest to talk about going to the psychiatrist. He felt it was a weakness. A character flaw. An admission of inadequacy. Another failure. *"You were the go-to guy.* You go to a shrink, you're mentally ill." It was okay to see an internist about high blood pressure. That was a respectable illness. Mental illness wasn't respectable. You were just another nut case. If word got out at the corporation, they'd think he was unreliable. He'd be washed up. He just needed to buck-up. Get hold of himself. Take control. Ernest looked at Mary. "He asked me when I last had a good day."

"What did you tell him?"

"Six months ago on the golf course. I shot two birdies."

Mary waited. Afraid to push.

"He said I should have had a good day in the last three or four days. He thinks I'm depressed." Ernest frowned. "I'm not depressed. I just feel low. People feel low. Things happen." He glanced accusingly at Mary. "You're not always chipper." He was quiet a while. "He thinks I should take medication." Ernest stood, hands in his pockets and paced the room. "I'm not sick. I'm in a slump."

"What would it hurt to try some medicine? He knows about these things. It's his job."

"Nobody knows their job," Ernest growled.

"He's a doctor!"

"If I take medicine, it means I'm sick."

"But it might help you."

"Mary, sometimes I think I *should* feel bad. I've left some wreckage in my wake. People pay for their mistakes."

"I want my old Ernie back." Mary paused. "Don't you want the old Ernie back?"

"Maybe this is the real Ernie." He poked himself in his chest and stared out the window. Finally, he sat down across from her. "I keep seeing that TV ad with the egg in the frying pan: 'This is your brain on drugs.'"

"You know better than that. Medicines aren't street drugs."

"If I take medicine, maybe I won't be me anymore. Maybe I'll lose something of myself. Maybe my ability to think and work will fizzle out. I like my cynicism. What if I lose my edge? What if I become a sweet, simpering idiot?"

Mary took his hand. "Ernie, I love you, but it can't go on like this." Tears welled up in her eyes. "You're terribly unhappy. It spills over on everyone. You're not just hurting yourself. You're hurting your friends. You're hurting me. Take the medicine. Please. For me, if not for you. Just try it…"

CHAPTER FIVE

The Psychological Disease

Save me, O God,
for the waters have come up to my neck.
I sink in deep mire,
where there is no foothold;
I have come into deep waters,
and the flood sweeps over me.
I am weary with my crying;
my throat is parched.
My eyes grow dim
with waiting for my God...
Do not let the flood sweep over me,
or the deep swallow me up,
or the Pit close its mouth over me...
I am lowly and in pain.

PSALM 69:1–3, 15, 29a

A psychologist to whom we refer people from time to time tells us 60 percent of her clients are suffering from some form of depression. This is not an unusually high percentage. She also tells us that many of her patients have more than one illness (doctors call this co-morbidity). In other words, a person suffering from depression may also have other medical or psychological diseases.

What Is a Psychological Disease?

Humans are more than the sum of their parts. As we have seen, the brain is anatomy, chemistry, hormones, and instincts, but our minds (psyches) function far beyond these biological dimensions. We are able to think in ways that transcend our biology. We process information, formulate ideas, experience emotions, establish values, assign meanings, create art, and order our lives in terms of goals, hopes, fears, beliefs, relationships, and social constructs. We make choices or judgments that give our lives purpose and emotional satisfaction.

When we suffer depression, these psychological dimensions of our humanity become warped. These disturbances manifest themselves on a continuum that can range from "life is not working very well" to profound psychosis (psychological disease that results in a break with reality). One hundred years ago William James spoke of this kind of continuum in *The Varieties of Religious Experience*. He said depression can manifest itself as "mere passive joylessness and dreariness, discouragement, dejection, lack of taste and zest and spring" for life.[1] He calls this form of depression *anhedonia*–the loss of appetite for all life's values and pleasures. The other end of the spectrum is not simply the "incapacity for joyous feelings, but positive and active anguish." Active anguish includes loathing, irritation and exasperation, self-mistrust, self-despair, suspicion, anxiety, trepidation, and fear. These psychological dynamics fill one with horror, a kind of desolation that is absolute and complete.

When we speak of depression as a physical disease, a psychological disease, a social disease, and a spiritual disease, we do not mean to convey that these are separate categories of depression. Rather, there are physical, psychological, social, and spiritual dimensions in depression. The psychological aspects of depression can be addressed through the use of medication and also through some form of psychological therapy. Psychology is a non-medicinal discipline devoted to the study of the mind (not simply the brain) and human behavior in individuals and groups. Psychologists often use various testing techniques that help analyze human behavior. Tests are usually "pencil and paper" tests that help classify the client's experience of depression and establish a diagnosis and develop treatment plans. Psychologists then use talk therapy to address behavioral, emotional, relational, and educational issues. Psychologists aren't licensed to prescribe controlled medications.

What Can a Psychologist Do?

We have established some broad parameters about the causes of depression and how it affects all aspects of living. We believe that ideal treatment is a collaborative effort that combines the skills of various therapists using the tools from their several disciplines. When a person finally confronts the reality that he or she is depressed, it creates conflicted emotions–relief, denial, embarrassment, uncertainty, and anxiety–and sends them reeling. They need

---

[1]William James, *The Varieties of Religious Experience* (Cambridge, Mass.: Harvard University Press, 1985), 123ff.

understanding, information, education, and guidance. The root biological cause of depression must be addressed with medication and ancillary medical therapies. However, with regard to psychotherapy, general physicians usually don't have adequate time because of busy schedules. Even psychiatrists may not focus on or commit the time necessary for psychotherapy. A psychologist, by training and professional purpose, is ideally suited to provide education, support, insight, objectivity, feedback, understanding, and guidance. A person suffering from depression can, in the presence of a good psychologist, begin the process of understanding what is happening, come to terms with feelings and fears, make emotional adjustments, develop coping strategies, address certain habits and behaviors, deal with relational issues, and find the means for exploring the future with hope.

Among the reasons for combining medication with psychological therapy is that while medication treats the biological disease, counseling can address interpersonal relationships and the social environment. People don't live in isolation but in a matrix of family relationships and social systems. The depressed person impacts these relationships and systems and, in turn, is affected by them. A good psychologist works in coordination with other health professionals and support groups, and empowers the depressed patient to find wholeness and health. In addition to the varied skills the psychologist brings to therapy, talking reduces stress. It's as simple as that.

Goals of Psychotherapy

■ Coordinate treatment plans.

■ Explain what other health professionals can provide.

■ Help clients set goals for their therapy.

■ Help the person suffering from depression understand the disease. Decisions can be based on knowledge rather than ignorance, irrational fears, anger, and frustration.

■ Develop buffers against depression: good nutrition, appropriate exercise, adequate sleep, better communication skills. Also establish healthy ways to recognize and meet emotional needs.

■ Help prepare a person emotionally for the possibility of the trial and error that is often connected to finding the appropriate medication that is most effective for that person.

■ Encourage compliance in taking medication and provide support in dealing with possible side effects.

■ Help the patient make behavioral changes that stick, including breaking destructive habits and establishing new patterns of effective coping that bring lasting change.

■ Explore issues that may surround the depressive episode—past abuse, attention deficit disorders, alcohol and drug abuse, anxiety and personality disorders.

■ Help the patient come to terms with past events that affect present thinking and behavior.

■ Deal with safety issues such as suicide prevention.

■ Explore new life situations and social relationships.

■ Help define and articulate problems, feelings, and issues arising from depression.

■ Help identify major sources of stress and initiate actions to eliminate or reduce them.

■ Identify and eliminate or reduce "triggers" for depression.

■ Help deal with more than one illness (co-morbidity): a diagnosis of cancer or recent heart problems, alcohol and drug abuse. Co-morbidity must be addressed. A patient cannot recover from depression and abuse alcohol.

■ Help create and recognize small successes in therapy that can be a foundation for future successes.

■ Help prevent relapses into depression, including helping the client monitor moods and mood swings.

■ Be available to family members who are affected by the presence of depression in a family system.

■ Deal with stigmas that clients fear are attached to a diagnosis of depression.

■ Help sort out the maze of questions regarding health insurance and psychological care.

It is important to recognize that over the past half century many specialized forms of psychological therapy have been researched, developed, and applied to mental health issues. This is particularly true in treating depression. People seeking psychotherapy are not limited to classical psychoanalysis and in-depth psychology. New therapies include both individual counseling and group psychotherapy and support.

Some Psychological Therapies

There are many therapeutic methods in psychotherapy. *Most therapists are not "purists," but are eclectic in their approach, and include a number of different therapeutic methods tailored to the specific needs of the client.* What follows is a discussion of classic therapeutic modalities.

Cognitive Therapy

This approach was developed in the 1960s and has proven remarkably helpful in treating the symptoms of depression. It is based on the understanding that serious episodes of depression are experienced by people who have a distorted view of themselves and the world. This distorted view is based in negative thoughts about themselves and their world. These habitually negative thought patterns perpetuate the depressive episode and cloud the person's view of reality. The triangle of negative thinking includes:

■ Negative thought about one's own self and personhood.

■ Negative interpretation of life's experiences.

■ Negative thoughts about the future.

William James wrote of the negative and melancholy outlook on life and contrasted what he called "healthy-mindedness" with "sick-soulness." The

> healthy minded live habitually on the sunny side of their misery line; the depressed and melancholy live beyond it, in darkness and apprehension…There are men who seem to have started in life with a bottle or two of champagne inscribed to their credit; whilst others seem to have been born close to the pain-threshold, which the lightest irritants fatally send them over… In short, life and its negation are beaten up inextricably together…The breath of the sepulcher surrounds it…Unsuspectedly from the bottom of every fountain of pleasure, as the old poet said, something bitter rises up: a touch of nausea, a falling dead of the delight, a whiff of melancholy, things that sound a knell…There is a pitch of unhappiness so great that the goods of nature may be entirely forgotten, and all sentiment of their existence vanish from the mental field. For this extremity of pessimism to be reached, something more is needed than observation of life and reflection on death. The individual must in his own person become the prey of a pathological melancholy. As the healthy-minded enthusiast succeeds in ignoring evil's very

existence, so the subject of melancholy is forced in spite of himself to ignore…all good…For him it may no longer have the least reality.[2]

For the person locked in negative thought patterns, the grinning skeleton is always seated at the banquet!

Cognitive therapy is designed to recast a person's habitual negative thinking and maladaptive behavior. The goal is not to have the client adopt a "Pollyanna" view of life, but rather to move the client from a completely negative view of the self and the world to more realistic thought patterns. This therapeutic approach deals with the "here and now" of a person's life and addresses immediate problems in such a way as to break recurring negative thought patterns and the depressive emotions they foster in a relatively short period of time. It also involves an educational process that helps the client to monitor his or her own thought patterns and to modify them.

Psychoanalytic Psychotherapies

Classical psychoanalysis as developed by Freud and his disciples usually involves several therapy sessions a week over an extended period of time. This kind of therapy is based on the belief that current psychological problems are the result of repressed memories and feelings from the past. These repressed memories and feelings reside in the unconscious part of the mind and they surface into conscious life, creating psychological problems. This approach to therapy is more likely to be used when a person has a long history of depression and the causes of the depression are not readily apparent. Psychoanalysis involves a client freely talking about past experiences, recalling painful events and the emotions associated with them. The psychoanalyst or therapist helps the client interpret and come to terms with his or her psychological history and problems. There are new psychoanalytic therapies that take less time than classic Freudian analysis.

Interpersonal Therapies

This approach to psychological treatment is based on the belief that depression is often made worse by interpersonal problems in social relationships. It deals with unhappy relationships and the emotional stresses that accompany them. The therapy is directed at the here-and-now of a person's life, as is the case with cognitive therapy, and is designed to deal with symptoms in a relatively short

---

[2]Ibid., 115–22.

period of time. Interpersonal therapies help the client with problems in social settings by developing coping mechanisms and social skills to repair or strengthen family ties, friendships, and working relationships. Clients are taught how to defuse confrontational situations with practical advice on what to say and do.

Behavioral Therapies

This therapy is an outgrowth of psychological behaviorism, a belief that our behaviors, emotions, moods, and reactions are learned and conditioned (Pavlov's dog). Based on this theory, what we have "learned" can be "unlearned" and our "conditioned responses" can be "re-conditioned." Some destructive behaviors are physiologically addictive (drug abuse). Others are psychologically habit forming (verbal abuse). Often they are both. Admittedly, behaviors that are central to a lifestyle are hard to change, but behavior therapy focuses on unlearning old dysfunctional behaviors and learning new and healthier behaviors. Since people can sometimes act their way into new ways of thinking more easily than they can think their way into new ways of acting, new behaviors can lead to new and healthier emotions. Treating destructive behavior treats depression. Conversely, treating depression treats addictive, destructive behavior.

Client-centered Therapies

Carl Rogers was a pioneer in client-centered counseling and this approach to therapy is sometimes called Rogerian. He emphasized that true and lasting change in a person's life comes about through "experience in a relationship." This therapy is grounded in the therapist building a relationship of respect and understanding with the client. The therapist is nondirective (doesn't interpret psychological events or emotions or direct the client toward a certain action), but helps the client clarify feelings and thoughts and promotes a sense of self-esteem. Positive regard for the client is a hallmark of this approach, but that of course should be the hallmark of any therapy.

Pastoral Counseling

This specialized form of counseling is done by ordained clergy with advanced training in pastoral psychotherapy. Pastoral counseling is unique because it combines psychotherapeutic methods with the healing resources of the Judeo-Christian tradition. Issues at the intersection of religion and mental health can be explored. Just as there are good and bad doctors, there is good and bad religion (as well as good and bad pastoral counselors). Good religion and good pastoral counselors provide resources that are in themselves healing, bringing a profound sense of hope. Bad religion and bad pastoral counselors increase pathology, create dependency, and block wholeness.

Most ordained clergy have a liberal arts bachelor's degree and a master of divinity degree. This is a three-year master's degree during which studies are conducted in the biblical, theological, historical, and ethical disciplines of the church, as well as the disciplines of pastoral care, counseling, philosophy, and the psychology of religion. Most pastors have received clinical pastoral education training in general or mental hospitals. This training focuses on dealing with people in crisis, combining the disciplines of theology, psychology, and the psychosocial sciences. Clergy who specialize in pastoral counseling have done post-seminary training and many have received a doctor of ministry degree with an emphasis in counseling. You can find qualified pastoral counseling through the following:

■ The American Association of Pastoral Counselors

■ The Association of Clinical Pastoral Education

■ The Canadian Association for Pastoral Practice and Education

■ The College of Pastoral Supervision and Psychotherapy

■ The Association of Professional Chaplains

■ The National Association of Jewish Chaplains

■ The National Institute of Business and Industrial Chaplains

Group Therapies

Human beings are social creatures and spend most of their lives in various groups. Psychotherapy is often conducted with small groups. The therapist uses various therapeutic modalities to facilitate discussions in which individual persons can learn coping and problem-solving skills. If the group is centered on a particular issue (alcoholism, spousal abuse, compulsive gambling, depression), it serves as a means of powerful support. Biases, stigmas, myths, fears, and shame are dealt with. There is opportunity to confront accusations of weakness, laziness, and character defects. Groups are a safe place to find help, support, and hope. People learn that they are not alone.

Family Therapies

Family therapy is group therapy focused on the family and its individual members. Families and individual persons don't get sick by themselves and they don't get well by themselves. When one member of the family has problems, it creates problems within the family. Family therapy can be directed at the following issues:

■ Determine if a family member is carrying unacceptable emotional burdens for the entire family.

■ Enable family members to be both individuals and family members.

■ Define boundaries between family members, clarifying roles and functions and allowing all members to realize their full potential.

■ Foster equitable solutions to power imbalances within the family when a family member is excessively controlling.

Expectations of Therapy

Therapy will never solve all of a person's problems because problems are part of living. The person with no problems or stress isn't doing anything and has no life of substance. Even Sigmund Freud felt that the goal of psychoanalysis was to turn neurotic misery into everyday suffering. That may sound pessimistic, but to move beyond neurosis to having choices and options is no small thing. Most depressed people, with proper therapy, will improve within two to three months, perhaps sooner. The remainder should improve within the year. Treatment should be continued for whatever length of time is necessary, and since depression, like other illnesses, can be chronic and recurrent, therapy may be needed throughout the person's life. Depressed persons may need evaluation and "tune-ups," just like an arthritis or high blood-pressure patient. A depressed person, in the context of his or her support system, must cooperate with health-care professionals in a treatment plan. Doctors call this patient-compliance. Failed therapy in disease, including depression, often occurs simply because the patient stops taking her or his medication or doesn't keep appointments with therapists.

You and Your Therapist

Perhaps the most important issue to be addressed in talk therapy is not the method of therapy, but the relationship between the therapist and the client. This involves the personalities of both parties, the level of trust that is perceived, and the success in forging a relationship. Studies of therapeutic relationships reveal that the most important factor in successful therapy is client motivation for change. The second is the therapist's personal attributes. A distant third is therapeutic modalities and technique. In other words, successful psychotherapy depends largely on a client's desire to get better and on the existence of a good chemistry between the client and the therapist. Indeed, the client-therapist relationship may be the single most important curative factor in psychotherapy or counseling.

Choosing a Therapist

We begin with the assumption that a diagnosis of depression has been made, or is at least under consideration, and the person suffering from depression accepts the need for treatment. It's not always easy to know where to begin. Where should I look for help? To whom should I talk? Do I need to see a physician? Do I need to see a psychiatrist? Should I talk with a psychologist? Should I go see my pastor?

There are two pressing needs for a person suffering from depression. Somewhere, early in diagnosis and therapy, it's important to see a medical doctor. It can be a family physician, internal medicine specialist, or a psychiatrist, but a thorough physical examination is necessary to establish that there are no medical illnesses present with depression (co-morbidity) and that no disease is present whose symptoms can mimic depression. For those who resist seeking treatment for depression as a mental illness, the physical examination may provide a "back door" to treatment. The other need is for some form of counseling or psychotherapy that helps educate and provides insight and support for a successful treatment program. Since medication and psychotherapy often go hand in hand, the following suggestions may help you begin the journey to wholeness and health.

Begin with those with whom you are already familiar and have some relationship. This most probably will be your family physician or your pastor. Your physician already has some idea of your medical history and will be able to conduct a physical examination. Your physician will be able to prescribe medication, will be aware of medications you are currently taking, and will be able to refer you to other health professionals, including psychiatrists and psychologists. You may feel more comfortable seeing a psychiatrist initially. Your pastor has some understanding of your life situation, your spiritual/ emotional history, and your relationships. Your pastor should be able to refer you to other health professionals. Keep in mind several things as you search for a therapist:

■ When you first see a psychologist or psychotherapist, satisfy yourself that you feel like you are in competent hands. Ask questions concerning his or her training, background, therapeutic approach, clinical experience, and memberships in professional organizations.

■ Explore the therapist's willingness to use a team approach (physicians, psychiatrists, pastors, other counselors, and health professionals) to therapy and ask what experiences they have had in such a collaborative effort.

■ Trust your intuition about whether you are able to talk with and form a good relationship with the therapist.

■ Ask if the therapist recognizes biological and chemical origins of depression and what his or her attitude is toward medication.

■ Ask if the therapist is available to family members, with your permission, to discuss nonconfidential issues and questions regarding treatment, progress, needs, and goals.

■ If at all possible, choose a therapist with whom you do not have a dual relationship (someone you see in other social settings) that might create conflicting boundary issues.

■ Ask the therapist what your therapy would entail and inquire about realistic goals and length of treatment.

■ Ask about costs, insurance, and financial arrangements.

■ If you don't feel comfortable with the responses, see another therapist. You must find the right "fit" for you.

If you are unsure where to begin, telephone your state or county psychological association. They will have a referral line that will provide you with a list of licensed psychologists in your immediate area. Be aware of the following distinctions:

■ **Medical Doctor (M.D.):** a graduate from medical school who has passed national or state board examinations. Some M.D.'s specialize in family medicine, while others have specialties such as internal medicine, various surgical fields, pediatrics, psychiatry, and so on (all of which require post-graduate residency programs of at least three years). Medical doctors can write prescriptions for medications.

■ **Doctor of Osteopathy (D.O.):** a graduate of an osteopathic medical school who has passed national or state board examinations. Doctors of osteopathy have the same general training as M.D.'s, sometimes emphasize body manipulation as part of therapy, and also have specialties requiring post-graduate residency training. Historical distinctions between M.D.'s and D.O.'s have been blurred in recent years and both perform the same general functions and share privileges at the same hospitals. Doctors of osteopathy can also write prescriptions for medication.

■ **Psychiatrist:** a medical doctor with a specialty in psychiatry. Some psychiatrists have subspecialties in particular aspects of psychiatry such as child or geriatric psychiatry. Most psychiatrists are associated with general or mental hospitals, and can hospitalize patients to manage severe mental illness.

■ **Psychologist:** a psychologist has a degree in psychology. This could be a bachelor's, master's, or doctor's degree, and one should be aware of the differences in these levels of education and training. A psychologist who is certified by the American Board of Professional Psychology has a doctoral degree, a number of years of clinical experience, has successfully completed standard national examinations, and is licensed by the state. Doctors in psychology may have a Ph.D. (Doctor of Philosophy), Ed.D. (Doctor of Education), or a Psy.D. (Doctor of Psychology with emphasis in clinical training and counseling). As previously mentioned, psychologists cannot prescribe medication and they work collaboratively with psychiatrists and other medical doctors who are licensed to prescribe.

■ **Psychotherapist:** Many practicing therapists use this term, and those using it range from a highly skilled medical doctor, psychoanalyst, or psychologist with years of clinical experience to someone who is a recent college graduate with a B.A. (Bachelor of Arts) degree in psychology to a New-Age guru. The term *psychotherapist* is as generic as the term *consultant.* It can cover different educational backgrounds and experience, or very slim credentials might underly the use of the term. Therefore, ask questions of the therapist during the initial interview.

■ **Social Worker:** Social workers assist persons in the context of their life situations and specific needs. A number of social workers are involved in the mental health field, and their education and experience vary widely. Some are in private practice; others are associated with mental health institutions. They provide counseling and community resource information. The letters B.S.W. designate a bachelor's degree in social work; M.S.W., a master's degree; and D.S.W., a doctor's degree. Most states license social workers and the credentialing may be designated L.C.S.W. (Licensed Clinical Social Worker), L.M.S.W. (Licensed Medical Social Worker), or B.C.S.W. (Bachelor of Clinical Social Work). Certification in the National Association of Social Workers depends on having a master's degree, two years of experience, and passing a national examination.

These descriptions are not meant to be exhaustive in their analysis of types of therapies and kinds of therapists. Rather, they are intended to serve as a guide to help you in your search for psychological support and treatment. Remember that you are the client (patient) and also the consumer of services. It is important that your choice of a therapist and therapy fit your own sensitivities, needs, and treatment goals. The genuine test of psychological therapy is whether it works for you and furthers health and wholeness.

There is much to drag us back, O Lord.
Empty pursuits, trivial pleasures, unworthy cares.
There is much to frighten us away;
Pride that makes us reluctant to accept help,
Cowardice that recoils from sharing your suffering;
Anguish at the prospect of confessing our sins to you.
But you are stronger than all these forces.
We call you our redeemer and savior because you
Redeem us from our empty, trivial existence,
You save us from our foolish fears.
This is your work which you have completed
And will continue to complete every moment.[3]

Søren Kierkegaard (1813–55)
Lutheran Christian and Existential Philosopher

---

[3] *The HarperCollins Book of Prayers,* comp. Robert Van de Weyer (Edison, N.J.: Castle Books, 1997), 230.

The Man Who Couldn't Dance: PART SIX

Ernest settled into a pew near the back of St. Thomas' Church. Mary had followed her own suggestion and was away visiting her parents. The bright sun of the winter day had warmed neither Ernest's body nor his spirit. The darkness of the sanctuary settled around his shoulders. The organ began the prelude and his uneasy heart thrummed with melancholy empathy to the overtones of the vibrating pipes.

Religious faith was deeply embedded in Ernest's life. He had grown up in a mainline Protestant church. The rational approach to faith seemed to make sense in the ordered world of his youth. He was a child and he understood as a child, he thought as a child, he spoke as a child. *Oh, God,* Ernest thought. *Childhood...*The wind, carrying the scent of earth and corn and rain, had been invigorating in its incessant sweep across the prairie that had been his home. He had a child's view of the world and it rang true. Now he was a man. He had put away childish things. The winds of experience blew across the landscape of his life—bending trees and rattling windows, stirring up dust devils and driving tumbleweeds into the fences that set the boundaries of his existence. It whistled through the desolate places of his soul. It blew with eerie sound and gusting force. He had turned his back to it, turned up his collar, and braced himself.

The world was no longer orderly. It was chaotic, confused, and unpredictable. His orderly religion no longer sustained him. What good was a rational faith in an irrational world? What good was a child's faith in a world of meat eaters? He dropped out of church for a while, then went church shopping. He longed for sanctuary, for at least a safe place, if not answers, to his diminishing sense of well-being.

The fundamentalist churches offered answers. For him, the rules and regulations didn't coalesce into a worldview that informed his life. Perhaps he was too rational and felt he was asked to leave his mind in the vestibule when he took his body into the auditorium. Rules for life seemed strung together from Bible verses like beads on a string. It was a rosary that he was unable to recite because the solutions seemed too simple for his complex problems.

Ernest's life among the charismatic churches was short-lived. The charismatics were full of life and joy and affirmation. Jesus was a buddy, protector, motivator, financial guide, healer, and Savior all at the same time. Earnest had tried. He had spent hours in the prayer closet. He had signed on to become a prayer warrior. It didn't work. "You've got to pray hard!" he was admonished—*Whatever that meant,* Ernest thought. His brothers and sisters cited promises from scripture about "asking and receiving, seeking and finding, knocking and the door being opened." They enthused that the "prayer of a righteous man availed much!" That he "didn't receive because he didn't ask." *No doubt,* Ernest thought, *this was true.* They quoted the words of Jesus recorded by the apostle John: "He who follows me will never walk in darkness." Ernest was confirmed in his lack of righteousness. Clearly, he was an outsider in the world of these gifted people. Perhaps God didn't think he was worthy of a second work of grace or a special gift of the Holy Spirit. God had never seemed more distant or powerless. He was ashamed of his failed faith. He was guilty and weak. Perhaps God was punishing him.

Ernest felt more alienated from God. The mainline churches offered rationality. Fundamentalist churches offered answers. Charismatic churches offered magic. Free Bible churches offered slick, shake-and-bake religion that was shorn of history, tradition, and liturgy. Their brilliantly lit, happy churches suggested that religion was an enlightened state in which God was fully exposed and fully knowable. The euphoria and success they radiated didn't resonate with his soul. The promised land of peace, joy, and fulfillment soured in his imagination and became the broken-promise land. He had finally found his way into the Roman Catholic tradition, not because it was right and the other traditions wrong, but it suited him. The veil of shadows at St. Thomas was comforting. Ernest inhaled the incense and rested in the glow of candlelight that flickered across the icons.

The prelude came to an end and Ernest heard the priest intone, "In the name of the Father, and the Son, and the Holy Spirit. Amen." He attempted to focus on the unfolding liturgy. His sense of isolation bordered on panic. The darkness in the sanctuary seemed to merge with cosmic darkness. Visceral fear became irrational rage. He was lost, and he had lost things he could never recover. His dignity. The respect of his family and his friends. His courage. His gentleness. His self-respect. The zest he had once had for life. The humor had gone out of his life like an ocean tide, carrying with it all the passion. Not only the laughter, but the tears. He was a man who could neither dance nor weep.

Ernest knelt at the communion rail, cupping his hands as the sacrament approached. The communion wafer was pressed firmly into his hand. "The body of Christ given for you." Ernest ate. Nothing. No presence. No absolution. No hope. He moved away before the chalice was presented. No more sacrilege. The bloodless communion reflected the spiritual anemia of his life...

CHAPTER SIX

The Spiritual Dis-ease

You are the God in whom I take refuge;
why have you cast me off?
Why must I walk about mournfully
because of the oppression of the enemy...
Why are you cast down, O my soul,
and why are you disquieted within me?

PSALM 43:2, 5a

When you stretch out your hands,
I will hide my eyes from you;
even though you make many prayers,
I will not listen...
Come now, let us argue it out,
says the LORD.

ISAIAH 1:15, 18a

I do not understand my own actions. For I do not do what I
want, but I do the very thing I hate...I can will what is right, but
I cannot do it. For I do not do the good I want, but the evil I do
not want is what I do.

ROMANS 7:15, 18b–19

You will note that in the title of this chapter we have moved from using the word *disease* in speaking of depression to the word *dis-ease*. The grammatical hyphen points to a life (existential) reality. The physical, psychological, and social dimensions of depression come together in the spiritual dimension, which is where our humanity finds meaning and purpose in life. There is a universal religious thread woven into the fabric of human life. If you don't have an interest in the spiritual, you should probably lay this book aside.

In some sense, the study of religion is the study of ourselves. It addresses the issue of wisdom, or what has been called "delicious knowledge." Ludwig Feuerbach said, "Consciousness of God is self-consciousness...Knowledge of God is self-knowledge...Religion is the solemn unveiling of a man's hidden treasures, the revelation of his intimate thoughts, the open confession of his love-secrets."[1] Depression as a hyphenated spiritual dis-ease expresses the idea that human beings are separated and alienated, pilgrims far from home, uneasy in this present life. Just as the word *discourage* means our "courage has been taken away," so *dis-ease* indicates our ease has been taken away. Depression is a manifestation of this alienation and disaffection with ourselves, with others, and with God. Rubem Alves has characterized this issue powerfully when he says religion is not lost by abstaining from sacramental acts and not going to church, any more than sexual desire is eliminated by a vow of chastity:

> It is when pain knocks at the door, and technical resources are exhausted, that there is awakened among people the seers, the exorcists, the magicians, the healers, the 'blessers,' the priests, the prophets and poets, those who pray and supplicate without knowing for sure to whom. And then it is that the questions arise about the meaning of life and the meaning of death, questions from the times of insomnia and times before the mirror. What frequently occurs is that the same religious questions of the past are again articulated, but clothed now in secular symbols. The names have been metamorphosed. The same religious function persists. Therapeutic promises of individual peace, inner harmony, liberation from anguish, hopes for fraternal and just social orders, for the resolution of conflicts among persons, and for harmony with nature, however disguised they might be with the cosmetics of psychoanalytic/psychological jargon, or with the language of sociology, political science, and economics, will always be expressions of individual and social problems around which religious webs have been woven.[2]

None of this is to say that the pathological dimensions of depression don't need to be addressed with appropriate medical and psychological care, as we have made clear, but it is to call your

---

[1]Ludwig Feuerbach, *The Essence of Christianity*, trans. George Eliot (New York: Harper, 1957), 11, 12.
[2]Rubem Alves, *What Is Religion?* (Maryknoll, N.Y.: Orbis Books, 1981), 4–5.

attention to the significant religious/spiritual dimensions of depression and the role depression has historically played in spiritual struggles among religious people.

The Religious and the Dark Night of the Soul

Depression often raises difficult questions for the religious. If religion is understood to be about life and salvation, health and security, peace and joy, then depression can be experienced as negativity, judgment, sinfulness, lostness, and failure in the state of grace. In Nietzsche's sentiment, "Why don't the saved look like it?"[3] Or in the recent words of a parishioner, "If prayer is so powerful, why can't I pray my way out of depression?" Or again, in the words of eighteenth-century reformer Johann Starck (Lutheran Pietist and hymn writer):

> My God, you have plunged me into such sorrow and anguish that my eyes are swollen with tears, and even the beat of my heart is hard and irregular. Was I not happy once? Did I not enjoy peace and rest? I used to look to you for comfort and consolation. I used to flee into your arms when I was afraid. But now you yourself hurl me down; you yourself reject me. Indeed your rejection is the source of my anguish. At first I thought it was only my human friends who had turned against me; and I innocently believed that you would remain by my side. But then I found that you, my Divine Friend, are cold and indifferent. I tried to pray, but could feel no response. I cried out in pain, but my cries were lost in the empty sky.[4]

Or, finally, in the words of St. John of the Cross (Carmelite Friar, 1542–91), "O Lord, listen to my plea. With each new day comes death. I can no longer endure the darkness of my life. I die because I do not die."[5] There's not a book in the Bible or a century in the history of the church where one does not find expressions of this sense of spiritual desolation, and there's not a church or synagogue in the world where contemporary believers and worshipers do not echo this holy melancholy. Shakespeare expressed the experience for all humanity in Francisco's words, "'Tis bitter cold, and I am sick at heart."[6] A recent survey of ministers revealed that 64 percent of

---

[3]Friedrich Nietzsche, *The Portable Nietzsche,* ed. W. Kaufmann (New York: Viking Press, 1965), 204.

[4]Johann Starck, cited in *The HarperCollins Book of Prayers,* comp. Robert Van de Weyer (Edison, N.J.: Castle Books, 1997), 331.

[5]St. John of the Cross, *Dark Night of the Soul,* cited in ibid., 213–14.

[6]William Shakespeare, *Hamlet,* Act 1, Scene 1.

the people who sought pastoral care from them were suffering from depression.[7] What are religious people to make of the sickness of the heart that makes life bitter cold?

The "dark night of the soul," a phrase popularized by St. John of the Cross in the sixteenth century, came to be understood as part of the spiritual journey, a purgative stage in which interest in the world is completely lost and spiritual anguish is felt as being completely alienated from God.[8] Neither this world nor the next holds any connection to one's life. *Accidie* was experienced by the desert fathers and mothers in the fourth and fifth centuries as a condition of sin in which one was dominated by boredom, weariness, absence of focus, and spiritual and physical exhaustion. It was called "the noonday demon." By the fifth century, *tristitia,* a spiritual state of dejection and rejection marked by deep sadness that rendered one helplessly and hopelessly fatigued in body and spirit, was identified as one of the seven deadly sins. A modern word that comes close to the meaning of *tristitia* is the word *ennui,* a state of weariness and dissatisfaction that renders one tired of and bored with life. Ignatius of Loyola, founder of the Jesuits in the sixteenth century, spoke of a spiritual condition known as the *desolations,* defined as a bleakness of the soul experienced as movement away from God. The desolations were understood to be part of the spiritual journey.[9]

With the coming of the Reformation, focus on "the seven deadly sins" diminished and Martin Luther wrote of the sinful human predicament rather than specific sins, but he, too, knew the experience of spiritual desolations and terrors. He called them *Anfechtungen,* a word difficult to translate but which literally means "to be fought at."[10] It is similar to the idea of "the noonday demon." At one point Luther wrote the following:

> I am utterly weary of life. I pray the Lord will come forthwith and carry me hence. Let him come, above all, with his last Judgment: I will stretch out my neck, the thunder will burst forth, and I shall be at rest. O God, grant that it may come without delay. I would readily eat up this necklace today [Luther was holding in his hands a necklace of white agates] for the

[7]Howard Stone, *Depression and Hope* (Minneapolis: Fortress Press, 1998), 3.

[8]For more information on John of the Cross, see *John of the Cross: Selected Writings,* ed. Kieran Kavanaugh (New York: Paulist Press, 1987).

[9]For more information on Ignatius, see *The Spiritual Exercises for St. Ignatius,* trans. Anthony Mottola (New York: Doubleday/Image Books, 1989).

[10]Stone, *Depression,* 27.

Judgment to come tomorrow. Rather than live forty years more,
I would give up my chance of Paradise.[11]

The Great Paradox

What is the deeply religious person to make of such "soul-sickness" within the spiritual experience? Is one to welcome it, try to ignore it, deny it, fight it? We suggest that one recognize it and attend to it. As we have said, there are only two things you can do about depression: acknowledge it and get help.

This brings us to the great paradox. We have been discussing depression as the enemy, the terrible opponent, the grim beast, the deadly disease, but people who actually attend to their depression and soul-sickness within the human spiritual journey may ultimately find that though depression is an enemy, it may serve a purpose. This paradox makes discussion of depression difficult, especially in a time of have-a-nice-day happy-talk and euphoric, smiling church sanctity. Depression among religious people must be addressed.

False Assumptions of Religious Optimism

We believe there has been a subversion of Christian thought in popular religious culture in the United States over the past half century. Many large and growing churches have espoused a view of humanity that focuses on goodness and glory, happiness and fulfillment, health and wealth, joy and excitement. Worship has been reduced to "show time." Serious consideration of the spiritual pilgrimage is made almost impossible by a thin patina of lightweight music, pop psychology, sermon sloganeering, instant spiritual gratification, and the gospel of totally fulfilled lives. Anyone whose life is troubled by "the dark night," "the noonday demon," or "the desolations" is encouraged to "give themselves more fully to the Lord." Some simply slink away into the shadows beyond the sight line of pastoral concerns. After all, they think, what growing and successful church needs "problems" or "downers" like me?

To be sure, hope is at the center of the Christian tradition. It is essential both to understanding the gospel and to living life. Without hope, we are indeed hopeless, but hope is not sunny optimism and vision is not positive thinking. Neither optimism nor pessimism belongs in Christian thought. What is vital is Christian realism—a

---

[11]Quoted in William James, *The Varieties of Religious Experience* (Cambridge, Mass.: Harvard University Press, 1985), 117.

realism that holds hope close to darkness. As John Donne said, "He brought light out of darkness, not out of lesser light."[12] Having embraced the culture of the American dream and a gospel of success, we have come to view any form of suffering, distress, anguish, discomfort, heart-hunger, and lack of gratification as something gone wrong. The dark realities of the desert soul-scape are viewed as either flaws in the system or flaws in character. Popular religion either denies the darkness and desolation or presumes to stymie it with a quick fix. We believe that depression needs treatment, but we believe just as strongly that the spiritual dimensions of depression need tending to through prayer, meditation, spiritual direction, pastoral care and counseling, and sensitive theological reflection. There are some psychic pains that cannot be medicated and some spiritual hungers that can never be fully satisfied. Christian theology that promotes total fulfillment actually stifles the human spirit and is deadly to the human soul. Humankind was never meant to be completely satiated or satisfied. Good religion addresses these issues with profound spiritual sensitivities and discerning pastoral theology. Bad religion is a fast skate on thin ice.

Humans create culture because there is more to us than biology, chemistry, and instincts. Desire and yearnings are what make us human. We have "eyes" in our "hearts," and so we love, paint, dance, sing, create, tell stories, cry, laugh, and hope. This creative yearning *does* nothing. It doesn't heal disease-causing microbes, doesn't feed the poor, and doesn't conquer death, but it's integral to life. It serves our humanity.

We are creatures of desire because we know there is an absence. We long for what is not present. We seek an order of love. When desire fades and yearning flags, when hope wears thin and passion withers, when the chill of the sepulcher frosts the windows of the heart, it's time, as spiritual beings, to pay attention. It's a time of opportunity, though terrifying and painful, for attending to the mystery of divine and demonic forces. Spiritual, even sacred, realities are at the center of our humanity. The dullest of us vaguely intuit their presence. The most foolish of us endeavor to repress or ignore them. The dark night of the soul for those who attend to it has been, historically, the environment for seeing authentic light. This difficult and frightening passage teaches us that something more has been let loose in our world than biology accounts for, religious optimism promises, or satiated gluttony offers.

---

[12]Cited by Dimitri Mihalas, *Depression and Spiritual Growth* (Wallingford, Pa.: Pendle Hill Publications, 1996), 26.

Paradox is at the center of the spiritual life. G.K. Chesterton described paradox as "truth standing on its head to gain attention."[13] Failure may lead to success. Weaknesses may usher in strength. Imperfection may be the path to improvement. Wounds may be the source of healing. Being lost may precede being found. Our dark night may be the precursor to an inviting dawn. The death knell may be a summons to a more authentic life.

The Hebrew Bible passes down the story of Jacob wrestling at the river Jabbok with an unknown assailant. (See Genesis 32.) Was it God? An angel? A river demon? Depression? We don't know. We only know that it was a horrific life-and-death struggle in the dead of night during which Jacob held on. When morning came, he was left with a limp, a new name, and a blessing. Superficial religious optimism shrinks from life's shadows where evil, suffering, estrangement, brokenness, despair, and melancholy lurk to grapple with the sojourner by the river Jabbok. This prevents the pilgrim from coming to terms with the deepest questions of human existence. Religious optimism subverts the spiritual journey. Its shallow water fails to plumb the depths of the genuine complexities of life. Human helplessness, with its paralyzing pain and fear, may open up a more profound understanding and place the key to coping with a more complicated life in our hands. We confront the presence and power of evil when seized by a life-and-death struggle with depression as a spiritual dis-ease. Not evil that has been defanged by religious happy-talk, but the grisly, bone-chilling, heart-stopping knowledge of the salivating beast closing in on its prey. Overwhelming, terrifying need makes scented optimism, intellectual muscle-flexing, and sweet consolations simply irrelevant and irreverent. In the abyss, all we can do is cry for help.[14]

Attending to the Spiritual Dis-ease

We believe a blessing can come from our own struggle in the dark night by the river Jabbok. If we avoid the darkness, we may miss the greatest opportunity available to us to know something of our lives being held in the presence (and absence) of God. It is there that we hang on, cry for help, and ask for a blessing. We may walk with a limp for the rest of our days, but we also may carry a new

---

[13]J. D. Douglas, "G.K. Chesteron, the Eccentric Prince of Paradox," *Christianity Today* (May 24, 1974), reprinted Aug. 27, 2001, found online at www.christianitytoday.com/ct/2001/135.

[14]See James, *Varieties*, 115–16 and 135, including his entire discussion of "sick soulness."

name and a new love. As Thornton Wilder reminds us, "In the army of love, only wounded soldiers can serve."[15]

If we are to know anything of a great city like London, New York, or Paris, we must leave the false, garish, neon boulevards, and wander the dark side streets where the true Londoners, New Yorkers, and Parisians live. That was true for the Hebrew children in their search for God. God revealed God's self in obscure moments when God was sought, found, and heard in darkness. In the Old Testament, we read the story of God's giving of the law on Mount Sinai. "Then the people stood at a distance, while Moses drew near to the thick darkness where God was" (Ex. 20:21). In the gospel story of Jesus' crucifixion (the ultimate declaration of faith that God is with us in suffering love), the text says, "Darkness came over the whole land until three in the afternoon. And about three o'clock Jesus cried with a loud voice…'My God, my God, why have you forsaken me?'" (Mt. 27:45–46). Here is the story of the noonday demon and the darkness that surrounds its work. Here is desolation, loneliness, terror, and the stench of death. Approaching the tangible darkness where God was ravaged on the cross is terrifying because it emphasizes the infinite distance not only between us and God but also between God and God. This dark-night-of-the-soul distance is *God-forsakenness.* Alas, when we are confronted with stories of revelation in the darkness indwelled by God, we tend to draw back, run away, or hide. However, when we pay attention to this experience, we pay attention to ourselves and God. If we run from it, we may have no real interest in God, only a pious fascination with the "idea" of God.

The Rev. Dr. Kenneth Leech, spiritual director and activist Anglican priest in London's East End, powerfully addresses this issue of "God dwelling in the darkness." His insights, like those of other spiritual directors, provide enormous encouragement to those who are willing to attend to the darkness and dis-ease in their deeply human journeys.

> One of the central features of the understanding of God in the Jewish and Christian tradition is its insistence that God cannot be known directly. Only the idols can be known directly. They can be looked at, objectified, brought under our control. They are the tame gods, the gods of the status quo, the gods who know their place…The true and living God is known only in the consuming fire of the burning bush, the

---

[15]Thornton Wilder, *The Angel That Troubled the Water.*

thick darkness of Sinai, the thick darkness of Calvary. Only by entering into this darkness can we come to know God and ourselves. Only by entering the darkness can we recognize the light which shines precisely for this darkness. It is a step out of security into the 'night sky of the Lord.' Only by staying with the darkness does it become aglow with the divine glory.[16]

Leech's point, and the point of spiritual direction in attending to the dis-ease of depression, is that there is no future in trying to evade the darkness. He encourages us, in these most desperate moments of our existence, to enter into a profound interior encounter with the reality of the cross as the center of Christian faith.

> The cross stands between human falseness and human fulfillment, between dust and glory, between Eden and the new Jerusalem. And yet we know only too well that these are not different places: for sin and grace, hate and love, dust and glory, Eden and Jerusalem, go right through the middle of us and of our communities. Christ's cross meets us at that point of conflict of our own fragmentation and tension towards the new. It is at the point of our most profound brokenness, at the shaking of the foundations of our being, that Christ's cross becomes for us a symbol of hope for the reversal of the forces of death.[17]

The fundamental religious question is really a terrified cry, "Help!"[18] The answer is found in living the question, not avoiding or denying it.

The truth of our spiritual quest was captured by the seventeenth-century Anglican poet, John Donne:

> We think that Paradise and Calvary,
> Christ's cross and Adam's tree, stood in one place.
> Look, Lord, and see both Adams met in me.
> As the first Adam's sweat surrounds my face,
> May the second Adam's blood my soul embrace.[19]

---

[16]Kenneth Leech, *We Preach Christ Crucified* (London: Darton, Longman, and Todd, 1994), 83.

[17]Ibid. See also Kenneth Leech, *Subversive Orthodoxy* (Toronto, Ontario: Anglican Book Center, 1992), especially ch. 2, "Comfort or Transformation: The Crisis of Modern Spirituality."

[18]See James, *Varieties,* 135.

[19]Cited in Leech, *We Preach,* 98.

Thus, we must echo words written in the first chapter of this book. Like Adam, we know that we have been driven from the Garden. We live east of Eden, and an angel with a flaming sword guards our garden's gate. There are things we have lost and places to which we can never return. In facing our spiritual dis-ease in its various forms and degrees of severity, we must indisputably encounter it. It is a tragic loss to treat suffering as if something has simply gone awry. Spiritual maturity is not the accumulation of skills and techniques. It is not being transfigured into having problem-free lives. It comes through attending to and encountering the dis-ease and darkness of our own humanity. It comes "as a result of being opened up and confronted by realities which disturb and transform us: the reality of the Word of God, challenging, piercing, shaking us; the reality of the encounter with ourselves, with God, and with the depths in other people, through silence and darkness. Common to these encounters is the element of struggle, of conflict. We are formed through struggle."[20] Further, the "spiritual life is not a way of tranquilizing oneself against the world."[21]

> The dark night is in fact the way of illumination…The dark night is a process of dis-illusionment, of ridding oneself from illusions. The spiritual journey moves from the head to the deepest regions of the Personality…We lose control, and at times seem to be on the verge of disintegration. Yet through this experience of darkness we come to see more clearly; we come to love more fiercely; we become more truly human. The path through darkness is, in fact, the way of integration.[22]

Discernment is a necessary stage on our journey toward authentic humanity and knowing the love of God. The Greek word *diakrisis* reflects the historical tradition of attending to the spiritual dimensions of depression through discernment. *Dia* is a Greek preposition that means "through." *Krisis* is the Greek word for judgment, often conveying condemnation, separation, and punishment. We can see its relationship to the English word *crisis*. To attend to the crisis of the dark night of the soul is not to run from it, deny it, or fix it, but to find a way *through the crisis. Diakrisis* is used in 1 Corinthians 12:10 to

---

[20]Kenneth Leech, *Spirituality and Pastoral Care* (London: Sheldon Press, 1986), 31.
[21]Ibid., 33.
[22]Ibid., 23–24.

mean being skilled in discerning between good and evil in the discourse about life. It is through *diakrisis* that discernment, illumination, and integration can be restored to our lives and put us in touch with our spiritual center. It is a way to freedom from disintegration. It is a way to illuminate our own lives and the nature of the world we occupy. Attending to spiritual dis-ease can be a way to wholeness, reality, and redemption. As with the demoniac in Mark's gospel, it leaves us "clothed and in our right mind."

Salvation and Therapy

This brings us to the meaning of salvation and its relationship to therapy. We said in chapter 1 that there are a number of biblical words related to the concept of health and salvation. They all carry the idea of wholeness, soundness, and safety. Yet, there are differences. *Sozo* is not *therapeuo*; salvation is not therapy. Not all psychologies carry a full awareness of Christian values. Yet, in dealing with the whole person and dis-ease, we need both the dynamics and content of faith as well as the insight of science. In some circles, Christians have been taught to fear the sciences, especially the sciences of the mind. We want you to know that medicine and theology, psychology and faith, philosophy and religion can and do sit at the same table for nourishment and conversation. Each discipline brings its unique flavor to the feast. As people of faith in the journey of life, we need all the scientific, empirical, and humanistic understandings of human beings available to us. We also need the dynamics of religion: sustaining faith, enabling love, hopeful yearning, accepting community, and saving knowledge. All relationships, including the relationship with ourselves and with God, are a mystery. Knowledge of ourselves and knowledge of God within this mystery are not the same thing, but they are deeply related.

Generally speaking, salvation is the experience of the presence of God within the great existential questions of life: bondage and freedom, meaninglessness and meaning, alienation and community, death and life. To be saved is to know that one's life now and forever is held in the eternal life and love of God. For the Christian, this is Christ-centered faith. Jesus has disclosed the fullness of our humanity and its destiny in relationship to God. This experience of the divine presence is the awareness that our life flows from God, in God, to God.

This phrase relating the experience of the divine presence to an awareness that our lives flow *"from, in,* and *to"* God, is also the acknowledgment that we live our lives in three frameworks of time—past, present, and future. The experience of depression is always related to one or more of these frameworks. Thomas Oden,[23] in a seminal work on the structures of awareness, addressed the human problem of living in despairing self-bondage to inauthenticity in these three frameworks of time. We may be in despairing bondage to our past guilt or shame. If all our yesterdays haunt us, there is no genuine freedom for today or tomorrow. The burden we carry becomes intolerable. Anticipation of a future that is valueless, empty, or meaningless produces within us an anxiety that becomes intolerable. When time takes on the dimension of "futurelessness" for us, we are in despairing bondage to anxiety. If our present living is marked by joylessness, pointlessness, or nonfulfillment, then we are in despairing bondage to boredom. We are truly "bored to death." In attending to the spiritual dis-ease of depression, it is necessary that we find freedom *from* past bondages, freedom *in* our present circumstances, and freedom *for* the future living of our days.

Depression affects and infects all our frameworks of time—past, present, and future. Attending to the spiritual dimensions of depression through spiritual direction in the framework of a story of salvation addresses all the modes of time in which we live and the forms of bondage that accompany them. Salvation is the story of being saved "from," saved "in," and saved "for." The spiritual realities of freedom, forgiveness, grace, acceptance, trust, hope, love, passion, purpose, and meaning lie at the center of attending to our experience of depression within the three frameworks of time through which we experience our lives.

The Christian tradition of good pastoral care has historically focused on healing, sustaining, guiding, and reconciling. These functions of pastoral care attend to our human limitations. They also seek out avenues of hope, liberation, transformation, and redemption. In terms of salvation, pastoral care doesn't legislate dogma, but attends to the particularities of each human life in all its brokenness, alienation, depression, evil, hopelessness, limitations, disappointments, and failures. Compassion is at the heart of the Christian gospel. Pastoral care concerns itself with restoring the soul to participation in the life and love of God that gives meaning to our human journey. Attending to spiritual dis-ease takes place in the midst of the struggles of daily life, but it does so with unabashed confession, affirmation, and

---

[23]Thomas Oden, *The Structure of Awareness* (Nashville: Abingdon Press, 1969), 187–91, 242–47.

mediation of the mysterious truth that at the heart of reality is a love that will not let us go. In this manner, pastoral care addresses not only disease and dis-ease, but ultimate concerns of human existence.

Sacramental Worship and the Community of Faith

Sacramental worship within the community of faith is integral to the spiritual work that addresses depression. The relationship between worship and pastoral care is found in three areas:

- The framework within which pastoral care is provided and worship is celebrated.

- The points at which pastoral care and worship intersect.

- The biblical view of humankind that establishes rhythms of life between the intensely personal and the social/communal.

To again use the musical analogy, worship is to pastoral care what an orchestra is to the individual musician. The orchestra provides a framework, a ritual, and a community that joins together in a public place for a concert that expresses the individual musician's art, identity, and passion. Worship, according to William Temple, quickens the conscience by the holiness of God, feeds the mind by the truth of God, purges the imagination by the beauty of God, and opens the heart to the love of God.[24] Pastoral care and worship, if understood as *nurture toward wholeness*, intersect with many common concerns. They address realities that diminish our humanity, keep us from freedom, and prevent personal and social health. True, healthy, sacramental worship explores many issues:

Memory	Wonder
Identity formation	Mystery
Rational thought	Emotion
Pursuit of truth	Social interaction
Understanding	Ordering of life
Ethics	Shaping a worldview
Confession	Clarifying a vocation in the world
Forgiveness	Seeking hope for the future

---

[24]Cited in Murdo Ewen MacDonald, *The Call to Obey* (London: Hodder and Stoughton, 1963), 162.

All of these realities are also the substance and subject of pastoral care in attending to spiritual dis-ease.

Liturgy is the church's public work of enacting its view of reality and commitments. The use of ritual not only provides alternative ways for expressing certain realities but also may provide the only way to express them. This is especially true of sacramental expressions in which the framework of worship is a critical part of pastoral care from a Christian perspective. It is a way of expressing who we are, who we are in our relationships, and who we are becoming—all issues addressed in effective pastoral care and spiritual direction. All things human—judgment, challenge, forgiveness, grace, sin, shame, suffering, healing, guilt, reverence, love, uncertainty, fear, hope, and purpose—belong to the language and symbols and realities of both worship and pastoral care. The Bible always connects the individual person to the community. When one weeps, all weep. When one rejoices, all rejoice. When one suffers, all suffer. When one celebrates, all celebrate. Pastoral care and spiritual direction take seriously the role of the community in relation to the individual person. Worship is one way that individual pain or joy can become a shared experience. It takes private grief and makes it a public concern. It takes personal joy and deepens it in communal celebration. This is especially true in liturgical events surrounding births, deaths, baptisms, confirmations, confessions, marriages, absolutions, illnesses, anointings of the sick, and times of reconciliation. The community affirms that we are not alone, provides practical help and support, helps us lean into the pain, and encourages a vision that takes us out of self-centered isolation and moves us toward a vocation of service and meaning. A community of faith helps people dream. It makes known the invisible God by the shape the congregation takes. It mediates the divine presence through food, beauty, architecture, symbol, art, and ritual. Awareness of the historical community (the lives of all the saints) provides companions in memory and hope, for these are people who have shared our common humanity, common struggle, common dis-ease, and common faith. Life in a community of faith joined together—with passion and compassion, lament and praise, grief and glory—in sacramental worship helps articulate our alienation from God and our desire for God. Community and worship are wondrous gifts to one suffering from depression.

Medication and Salvation

Discussion of depression as a spiritual dis-ease may have raised questions about why you should take medication or receive psychological therapy. We believe that medication treats the dysfunctional biology of depression and psychotherapy treats the mind in depression. Such therapy will restore the energy, strength, and interest one needs to engage the noonday demon and travel through the dark night of the soul. Medication and psychotherapy don't make you something you are not (a common fear), but enable you to become who you are. A central truth of that "becoming" involves addressing the spiritual dimension of your humanity. It involves Christian salvation. Salvation isn't about peace and tranquility. It's about experiencing the divine presence so the soul can be securely open in the upheaval that allows us to actually see the light in the darkness, the healing in the wound, and the redemption in the suffering. Out of that experience can come wholeness that lives in the love of God and serves the purposes of the love of God in the needs of others.

O Lord, listen to my plea.
With each new day comes death.
I can no longer endure the darkness of my life.
I die because I do not die.
For what purpose do I still draw breath?
The only purpose is to delay the pains of death,
But my life is as painful as death.

I die because I do not die.
To assuage my pain I gaze on you,
In the form of the holy bread and sacred wine.
But my heart sinks because I cannot see your face.

I die because I do not die.
If I look forward to the joy of heaven,
When I shall at last see you face to face,
My present pain at your absence grieves me more.
I die because I do not die.
Draw me out of death's lair,
Make me free to live in your sight.
At present my soul is as dark as night,
I die because I do not die.

Who but you, Lord, could bring sweetness in the midst of
    bitterness,
pleasure in the midst of torment?

How wonderful are the wounds in my soul,
Since the deeper the wound, the greater is the joy of healing.[25]

St. John of the Cross (1542–1591)
Carmelite Friar, Author, Dark Night of the Soul

---

[25] *The HarperCollins Book of Prayers,* comp. Robert Van de Weyer (Edison, N.J.: Castle Books, 1997), 215.

The Man Who Couldn't Dance: PART SEVEN

Ernest shut the door to his empty house and moved slowly through the shadows to his study. It was uniquely his room. The diplomas hung on the wall, as well as the photographs, honors, awards, and military decorations. He stood at his desk where the light streamed through a leaded glass window and fell across the polished mahogany surface, reflecting the fading light of the winter Sunday afternoon. Once, Ernest had thought of the illumination as light from heaven. He opened a drawer and stared at the pistol. He had purchased it at a pawnshop almost a year ago. It had been the brightest of spring days and he had wanted to kill himself. The 0.45—chosen perhaps unconsciously from the many weapons in the glass-covered case—had been worn by him as a sidearm decades ago in a different life. The loaded gun had remained concealed these many months beneath a desktop that held the mementos of his successful life—mementos that had no value and held out no hope.

Ernest hefted the weapon in his hand. Felt its weight. Its absolute authority. He ejected the clip. The dull, lead slug lay against the gleaming copper shell casing like a gap-toothed grin. It was not a demented smirk. It was a friendly, inviting smile. He flopped in his chair. The dying day turned to night. He pressed the clip against his lips, like the kiss of the fingertips before making the sign of the cross. He savored the cool metal and the acrid smell of cordite. Vietnam swept over him with a thin, coherent shiver. Now a lifetime ago, Vietnam seemed like the good old days. He laid the clip beside the pistol on his desk. His eyes played across them. He could once disassemble and assemble the weapon blindfolded. Pistol and clip, separated by the few inches on the desk, were useless. Ernest, blindfolded by life, contemplated assembling them for their lethal power...

CHAPTER SEVEN

The Terminal Disease

Job opened his mouth and cursed the day of his birth...
"Let the day perish in which I was born,
   and the night that said,
      'A man-child is conceived.'
Let that day be darkness!...
Let the stars of its dawn be dark;
   let it hope for light, but have none;
      may it not see the eyelids of the morning—
because it did not shut the doors of my mother's womb,
   and hide trouble from my eyes.

Why did I not die at birth,
   come forth from the womb and expire?...

Why is light given to one in misery,
   and life to the bitter in soul,
who long for death, but it does not come,
   and dig for it more than for hidden treasures;
who rejoice exceedingly,
   and are glad when they find the grave?"

JOB 3:1, 3–4a, 9–11, 20–22

People engage in risky behaviors. Why they do so is problematic. There are those who sky-dive, and those who do so from altitudes of 35,000 feet, which requires thermal clothing and self-contained oxygen. There are those who ride motorcycles and those who ride them without a helmet. There are those who drink and those who drink and drive. There are those who drive and those who drive Formula One race cars. There are those who hike and those who hike Mount Everest. We make jokes about having a death wish, but there are some people who do have a death wish and it's no joke.

And some, like Ernest, not only long for death but also make painstaking plans to take their own lives. Not all who make such plans act on them, but too many do. The ultimate destructive behavior, suicide is the unmentionable, unthinkable specter of death grinning in the wings that haunts a potential victim and hovers fearfully over that person's family. Suicide has a fatal allure for the very vulnerable as a way to solve problems that seem insolvable. Suicide also holds a morbid appeal—at once abhorrent and fascinating—for the healthy mind. Suicide has drawn the attention of theologians, the legal profession, physicians, psychologists, and sociologists.

Suicide has traditionally been regarded as a sin against God in the monotheistic religions—Judaism, Islam, and Christianity. Suicide is rare in the Old Testament, and by the second century, Talmudic writings inveighed against suicide and proscribed religious burial for suicide victims. Nevertheless, there are recorded instances of mass Jewish suicide during severe persecutions, which parallels thought that it is an acceptable solution in times of extremity and utter hopelessness (a presumption borne out by current epidemiological statistics—see pages 102–4). Curiously, Jewish suicide was uncommon during the Holocaust, and we know of no instances of mass suicide.

Islam traditionally condemns suicide based on the belief that only Allah determines destiny and death. The exception is suicide as a form of self-sacrifice in holy wars. Hinduism is more tolerant of suicide and accepts ritual suicide (*suttee*) by a widow as a praiseworthy solution to her plight and to discharge her spouse's debts. Shintoism regards suicide (*seppuku*) as honorable, especially among the warrior Samurai class.

The belief that suicide is a sin against God is embedded in historical Christianity, rooted in the conviction that it is a violation of the Sixth Commandment—"You shall not murder." Augustine (354–430 C.E.) condemned suicide as sin. The Second Roman Council of Orleans (533 C.E.) expressed the first official condemnation of suicide. Thomas Aquinas (1225–1274 C.E.) regarded suicide a sin. Pope John Paul II restated the Roman Church's condemnation of suicide in 1995, including it with opposition to euthanasia, abortion, and homicide. As such, suicide is regarded as the ultimate moral failing—perhaps even an unforgivable sin—since the victim, now dead, can no longer repent and receive absolution. Some editions of *The Book of Common Prayer* still mandate that the Order for the Burial of the Dead is not to be followed for those who have "laid violent hands upon themselves." At least one reason Hamlet didn't kill himself was his belief that God pronounced suicide a sin. Perhaps no one has ruminated on suicide more eloquently than the prince of Denmark:

O, that this too too solid flesh would melt
Thaw and resolve itself into a dew!
Or that the Everlasting had not fix'd
His canon 'gainst self-slaughter! O God! God!
How weary, stale, flat and unprofitable,
Seem to me all the uses of this world![1]

Suicide has been considered a crime in common law going back thousands of years. Suicide was regarded as an offense against the state in ancient Greece. Plato (427– 347 B.C.E.) condemned it as such. So did Aristotle (384–322 B.C.E.). Cicero (106–48 B.C.E.) condemned suicide, but considered it acceptable in matters of honor. Plutarch (46–120 C.E.) continued this Greek tradition. Suicide was not uncommon in Imperial Rome, and was considered an honorable choice among soldiers and the aristocracy. Suicide was often performed ritualistically in the company of friends and included food, drink, and final conversation. Still, Emperor Constantine I (290–337 C.E.) decreed strict laws against suicide, and the victim's property and goods were seized by the state. Rome officially criminalized suicide in the sixteenth century.

In the Middle Ages, in the emerging state theocracies, suicide was considered both a criminal act and a sin against God. The victim's corpse was often hung in the public square, mutilated, and ignominiously buried under a public thoroughfare. The victim's goods were confiscated by the courts. Suicide continued to be generally condemned until the latter part of the eighteenth century and the Enlightenment. Both theology and law began to argue that suicide was an irrational act and the suicide victim was neither morally condemned nor legally culpable. The link between suicide and "melancholy" was noted.

Civil law has been slow to reform suicide statutes and in some jurisdictions it is still listed as a crime. In Denmark, suicide was removed from the criminal statutes in 1866. England decriminalized suicide in 1961 (although punishment was abolished almost a century earlier), whereas suicide was a crime in Ireland until 1993. Criminalization of suicide in America would be governed by state law, and our research failed to find an American jurisdiction that made successful, unassisted suicide by an individual person that harmed no one else a criminal offense.

Whether or not suicide is regarded as a crime, such a death ensures the intervention of law enforcement agencies, the court system, and

---

[1]William Shakespeare, *Hamlet,* Act 1, Scene 2.

forensic pathologists. Usually it is readily apparent that the victim died by suicide, and this diagnosis is placed as the cause of death on the death certificate. Only rarely is there room for doubt, but in such cases, it is critical that the cause of death be identified. First, family and friends must know the truth if even some modicum of healing is to be possible. Further, certification of death by suicide, homicide, assassination, or accident has enormous implications in jurisprudence—mental competence, rights of inheritance, insurance claims, pensions, workman's compensation, medical malpractice, and product liability, to say nothing of retributive justice for the act of murder.

Physicians and psychologists seek to know the *why* of suicide. The physician author of this book was taught in his psychiatric training that suicide was meant to kill more than one person. However, at the very least, suicide is not only a violent act against the self but also a violent act against others. In the aftermath of suicide, family and friends suffer inconsolable grief, heartbreak, confusion, and pain. Medical research provides no simple, cogent explanations for suicide. Nor is there a reliable method to accurately predict who will commit suicide. Furthermore, suicide is commonly an ambivalent act: The victim wants both to live and to die.

Sociologists are fascinated by the *how, where*, and *when* of suicide. No one knows when the first hominid drew a sharp stone across his throat, jumped off a cliff, waded into a bog with no intention of returning, or, with deliberate self-destruction in the forefront of his mind, went out to face a saber-toothed tiger unarmed—perhaps our equivalent of "death by cop." Sociologists and epidemiologists have established that modern Homo sapiens choose the means at hand—firearms, pills, poisons, drowning, hanging, jumping. On occasion, the method is bizarre, grotesque, and even grisly. We recognize that some places are "suicide magnets": public monuments, buildings, bridges, and specific geographic sites. Sadly, almost 10 percent of suicides occur in psychiatric hospitals, the place where patients go to be safeguarded. Patients also are at higher risk for suicide on release from a hospital. An inadequate mental health program combined with an insurance system that mandates early discharge are partially responsible. In addition, the patient may be well enough to be discharged, but not well enough to function when released back into the family, social, and business environment that was overwhelming in the first place.

In sum, students of suicide have profiled susceptible medical conditions and personality traits tending toward suicide, and have discovered patterns in stages of life, methods, places, time of day or night, and seasons of the year. Still, the overriding question about suicide is always *why?* This question is never more acute for anyone than for the family. *Why, why, why?*

Suicide is surrounded by superstition and myth. Once again, epidemiologists have compiled statistics about suicide in the United States:

- Each year, 30,000 Americans die from suicide (one every seventeen minutes of every day).

- More Americans commit suicide each year than are victims of homicide.

- Suicide causes twice as many deaths each year as HIV/AIDS.

- Depression, manic-depression, and/or alcohol are involved in approximately 80 percent of suicides.

Several factors other than depression are linked to suicide:

- Other mental illness (schizophrenia)

- Drug and alcohol abuse

- Chronic pain

- Terminal illness

- Mimicry

Six factors increase the risk of suicide in a person with depression:

- The severity of the depression.

- Depression associated with delusions (fixed false ideas).

- Relapse into depression after treatment improves the patient's mood (increased energy may precipitate suicide if mental health and self-esteem have not improved significantly).

- Social isolation (unemployed, unmarried, and living alone).

- Alcohol and drug use. Alcohol lowers inhibitions, but alcoholics with depression have a higher incidence of suicide than alcoholics without depression.

- Access to a lethal means of suicide combined with impulsive behavior.

Research links adolescent suicide to hormonal changes of puberty, depression, and access to alcohol, drugs, and firearms in modern society. Each year twenty-five hundred adolescents commit suicide. Twenty-five percent of suicides are committed by people between ages sixteen and thirty, and 1 percent by people younger than sixteen. There are several risk factors in this age group:

- Depression (especially if you are male and depressed)

- Prior suicide attempts

- Alcohol and drug use

- Unwanted pregnancy

- History of physical or sexual abuse

- Unemployment

- Lack of social acceptance and struggles with sexual orientation

- Readily available means, especially firearms

Many other statistics about suicide are available:

- Suicide is the second leading cause of death among females aged 15 to 44.

- Suicide is the fourth leading cause of death in males aged fifteen to forty-four (after vehicular accidents, tuberculosis, and violence).

- Depressed males commit suicide four times more frequently than depressed females, despite the fact that twice as many women as men suffer from depression.

- More women make suicide *attempts* than men.

- Women tend to use less lethal means for suicide (overdoses or poisons as opposed to firearms).

- Twenty-five percent of those making a suicide attempt will repeat the attempt within the next twelve months.

- Following a suicide attempt there is a slightly increased risk that a future attempt will be successful.

- Fifty percent of successful suicides have no record of previous attempts.

- The age group at highest risk for suicide is the elderly. Suicide in this group is even more strongly associated with depression than among younger age groups.

■ Seventy-five percent of the elderly who commit suicide have seen a doctor within the previous month. (Physicians may miss a diagnosis of depression or warning signs of suicide, or it's possible that there is more physician-assisted suicide than formerly believed.)

■ The suicide rate for women age 40 is higher than the suicide rate for women age 75.

■ The suicide rate for women 75 years old or older is 5 per 100,000 population.

■ The suicide rate for men 75 years old or older is 37 per 100,000 population (about eight times the rate of women).

■ Ten percent of patients with manic-depression (Bipolar Disorder I) commit suicide, and just over 50 percent of these patients are male.

■ Eighty percent of people who plan suicide reveal their intentions to someone.

■ Caucasian Americans commit suicide at twice the rate of non-Caucasians, but the rate of suicide among African American males age 15 to 19 has doubled in the past two decades.

■ The risk of suicide is slightly increased within the nuclear family if a parent or other family member has committed suicide.

These statistics don't explain suicide or why people commit suicide. In some ways, they raise as many questions as they answer, but they do give us a point of departure for reflection. They reveal that causative factors in suicide include heredity, mental illness, an impulsive or violent personality, mimicry, and immediate social circumstances (failure or perceived failure, shame, romantic disappointment, financial setbacks, terminal and debilitating illness, and substance abuse). With exceptions so rare as to be almost non-existent, suicide is not the act of a healthy, rational person. For example, everyone experiences significant stress. Some thrive on it! Many suffer thwarted expectations, loss, failure, shame, serious illness, financial reversals, divorce, grief, heartbreak, and rejection in love. The overwhelming majority never even consider suicide as an option when confronted with reversal of fortune, let alone actually commit it. They pick themselves up and soldier on.

The *fundamental* causes of suicide are virtually always internal, not external. They lie within the labyrinthine recesses of the mind.

The normal brain is able to accurately interpret the environment, think logically, recognize options, and view the future with some hope. Failure to accomplish those mental tasks is a defining feature of mental illness—specifically depression. Depression lies at the heart of most suicides. The depressed brain, distorted by disease, views the future as bleak, barren, and barred to positive options.

Just as there is co-morbidity in physical illnesses (more than one disease in the same person), there is co-morbidity in suicide (more than one thing causes suicide). Some refer to this as the "multiple hit" theory. Depression is the most important "hit." As the hits stack up (impulsive personality, violent tendencies, serious personal reversals), they have a reverberating effect, looping back on themselves with ever-increasing urgency that may lead to suicide. When combined with substance abuse (prescription drugs, street drugs, or alcohol), these extra hits are deadly, and cumulative hits turn a vulnerable person into a tinderbox, awaiting only a chance spark to burst into flame. Under such conditions, suicide would almost seem inevitable. Although a disproportionate number of such persons do commit suicide, it is by no means inevitable. We wish to stress that most persons, in spite of multiple problems—including depression—don't take their own lives. If twenty million Americans suffer from depression in any single year and thirty thousand commit suicide, then well over 99 percent of depressed people don't kill themselves. The human species appears to be remarkably well-protected against self-destruction. It should be noted, however, that a half million Americans annually make suicide attempts serious enough to require emergency room care. Since depression often goes unrecognized and untreated, there is hope that much of this personal tragedy can be prevented.

Statistics are more useful in telling us who commits suicide and how and where, than in telling us why they do so. Why is it that some people reach a point in their lives where they believe life is no longer worth living?

Science and Suicide

Scientific research into suicide actually gives us very little data. We know serotonin plays a role in depression. It also plays a role in temperament. There is strong evidence from animal studies that high levels of serotonin inhibit violent, aggressive, and impulsive behavior. Studies in animal populations show that maternal and societal influences increase serotonin levels. Studies in human populations suggest that people who have low levels of serotonin are more impulsive. Brain tissue of suicide victims has lower levels of serotonin than brain tissue of people who die from other causes. Among a patient population (in Sweden) hospitalized for depression, six of the seven patients who later committed suicide had lower serotonin levels than the hospitalized patients who didn't later commit suicide. This scientific data, miniscule as it is, doesn't explain suicide biologically or fix a point where medical therapy might change suicidal thoughts. However, it can be said with some certainty that treatment for depression and manic-depression (Bipolar Disorder I) reduces the risk of suicide. Interestingly, Lithium reduces the rate of suicide in manic-depressive patients, but antidepressants do not.

Psychology and Suicide

Psychoanalysts have advanced a number of theories for suicide. Some theorize that suicide flows from the tension between the fear of life and the attraction of death. Sigmund Freud believed suicide was the result of aggression and unconscious conflict between the death instinct and the life instinct. Alfred Adler believed suicide grew out of an inferiority complex and that aggression was directed against both the "self" and people who were significant to the "self." Behavioral psychologists have advanced several suicide theories: Suicide is due to (1) Alienation and loss in social contexts; (2) Belief that death by suicide will advance a cause; (3) Abrupt changes in the life setting (negative—loss, with nothing to live for; positive—promotion, and a fear that the position is beyond the person's ability); (4) Abject fatalism (in prisoners, the oppressed, and terminally ill).

Preventing Suicide

Treatment for depression (and manic-depression) is the key to preventing suicide. Psychiatrists, psychologists, general physicians, pastors, priests, therapists, counselors, and educators should be able to recognize the psychopathology of depression in people who come to them for help. If they do not recognize and refer such persons for proper therapy, they allow them to continue on a course that may end in disaster. Family members, if attuned to signs of suicide, are also in an opportune position to intervene. Suicide mimicry occurs, but suicide clusters are a uniquely adolescent phenomenon. One adolescent suicide may prompt others within a close population, especially if they share risk factors. Adolescent suicide should prompt intervention by parents, school authorities, health professionals, and others suited to the task.

The following actions and attitudes are warning signs that a person is considering suicide:

■ Signs of depression (unrecognized and untreated)

■ Recovering from depression (energy levels rise and mobilization is increased)

■ Preoccupation with death

■ Talking about or threatening suicide

■ Expressions of hopelessness or worthlessness: "What's the use?" "People would be better off without me."

■ Making preparations for death (writing a will, giving away cherished possessions)

■ Planning suicide or obtaining means for suicide

■ Setting a deadline: "If I don't get this job"; "I'll give him one more chance."

■ Increasing or persistent alcohol or drug abuse

■ Chronic illness and chronic pain

When you observe these warning signs in a family member, friend, patient, client, parishioner, or student, take steps to intervene. Get help for anyone who threatens suicide or makes a suicide attempt (regardless of the flimsy means). Since those contemplating suicide often tell someone they are considering taking their own life, take them seriously. Subsequent denials don't mean they aren't going to do it. Some suicides are committed in an impulsive moment. Others carefully plan their suicides over weeks and months. Often, suicide is a mix of both planning and impulsive behavior. A sudden disappointment or frustration may precipitate the act of suicide, but the plan has been brewing for some time and the means have been acquired. Clinical depression, destructive behavior (substance abuse), and temperament (impulsiveness), when combined with a particular disappointment (break-up of a close relationship, a humiliating experience, loss of a loved one, loss of a job) may trigger suicide.

Things to Do When Someone Is Contemplating Suicide

Suicide *attempts* are a frightening and confusing event for family and friends. Suicide attempts may be rehearsals for suicide. Suicide attempts may be symbolic (a gesture). The attempt may be calculated to engender sympathy from the family or precipitate a crisis. Still, suicide threats or gestures must be taken seriously. At the same time, multiple threats or gestures serve ultimately to either desensitize the family (they no longer take the threats seriously) or alienate the family (they feel anger, frustration, fear). When you are afraid someone you know might commit suicide, or obliquely threatens suicide, you should take the following steps:

■ React calmly.

■ Ask about suicide. The fear of putting the idea into the person's head is not a real risk.

■ Take him or her seriously if suicide is mentioned or threatened.

■ Listen with concern. Don't immediately start talking.

■ Don't shrug off a suicide threat, no matter how trivial, and worse yet, don't laugh it off.

■ Don't say, "That's stupid," or "You've got to be kidding," or "You always…"

■ Don't offer platitudes or thoughtless optimism.

■ Offer empathy, maintain eye contact, comfort the person, embrace the person, or hold the person's hand (if appropriate).

■ Don't promise to keep the threat confidential or keep secrets.

■ Don't relieve the person of responsibility for his or her own actions.

■ Acknowledge that you can't handle the situation alone.

■ Get the person into treatment (a psychiatrist, psychologist, family physician, or emergency room). Don't just suggest treatment. Take him or her. Stay until a health professional has been seen. Supply the specific reasons you believe the person is suicidal. Wait. See if you can do anything else on the advice of the health professional.

■ Don't be talked out of intervention.

■ Don't debate moral issues, point out character flaws, or pronounce judgment.

■ Remove guns, poisons, pills, razors, ropes, and so on from the suicidal person's home or apartment.

■ Don't put your own safety at risk.

■ If an emergency exists, call 911.

■ Don't leave the person alone.

Remember, just as something that seems inconsequential can precipitate suicide, something that seems negligible (a supportive conversation) may prevent suicide.

Things to Say When Someone Is Contemplating Suicide

■ "You're not feeling down. Suicidal thinking is part of an illness. It's treatable."

■ "What do you have to lose by seeking help?"

■ "If treatment doesn't work, what have you lost?"

■ "Suicide is a permanent solution to problems that may seem insurmountable but can be overcome."

■ "You are responsible for your actions, and killing yourself would permanently harm your family and friends."

Raymond DePaulo, M.D., a psychiatrist at Johns Hopkins University School of Medicine, writes that he tells suicidal patients the following: "When you injure (or threaten to injure) yourself, it causes anyone who cares for you to pull back. These are the people you need most in your recovery. Your parents can't live with the constant fear that they will find you dead the next time they come home. All of us, even your doctors, find this too painful. Your family and your doctors have pledged not to give up on you. That's part of our responsibilities. Your responsibility, as a son or daughter (or father or mother), is to do everything you can to get well. This is your job— we can't really get you well without you doing your part. You expect me not to give up on you, well, I promise I won't, but then you can't give up either."[2]

One suggestion for protecting a suicidal person is to encourage the person (when rational) to create a "Ulysses Agreement" with therapists, family, and friends. Ulysses was the Greek character who asked to be lashed to the mast when his ship passed the island in the night so that he might resist the alluring call of the sirens. It might be possible to construct, with the patient's consent and input, a list of steps he or she wants taken if he or she is suicidal.

The damage from suicide is incalculable. Suicide takes the life of the victim, terminating a life with all of its possibilities. Suicide brings

---

[2]Raymond DePaulo, Jr., M.D., *Understanding Depression* (New York: John Wiley and Sons, Inc., 2002), 131.

immeasurable suffering to the people left behind–especially the immediate family. The effects ripple outward from the family to touch friends, schoolmates, coworkers, entire communities, and in these days of mass media, the world. Those who have committed suicide are beyond help. Survivors of the suicide victim aren't, and they need help. Most friends and family members of a suicide victim have asked in their hearts, if not aloud, "How could you have done this to me?" Or, "It was a thoughtless, cruel act!" Even though we tell ourselves that those who commit suicide aren't thinking rationally, in the disastrous moments and months and years following suicide the anguish for survivors is almost unbearable. They are left with both guilt and anger. They ruminate on the missed phone call. Or the call delayed, or not made. The cross words. The slights. They must sort out the good memories and the inevitable bad memories and deal with them. They must try to explain an inexplicable act. Above all, they are desperately sad and lonely, having lost someone with whom they were knitted together by golden threads of utmost intimacy.

Finally, in a paradox that is agonizing in its complexity, survivors often must deal with their sense of relief. Finally, they may think, it's over. No more burdensome, endless, painful, irresolvable, unhappy discussions. No more terrifying threats. No more searching out and removing means of suicide from the home. No more frantic telephone calls in the middle of the night. No more waiting for the call announcing the act that was both expected and dreaded.

Survivors experience an upheaval of conflicted feelings:

- Why did it happen?" The all-consuming, unanswerable question.

- Was it for revenge? "Was the suicide an act of vengeance because I...?"

- Guilt. "It's my fault..." "If I had been there..." "I should have known..."

- Shame. "Suicide is a weakness..." "Suicide is against God..." "Suicide is the unforgivable sin..."

- Disgrace. Suicide is felt to be a dishonorable death that is a blot on the victim's character.

- Stigma. Suicide is felt to reflect badly on both the victim and the family.

- Fear. "What if someone else in the family kills himself or herself?"

■ Posttraumatic stress syndrome may affect survivors, with its attendant nightmares, insomnia, and reliving of the event, especially if the survivor witnessed the act or discovered the victim.

Things to Avoid Saying to the Survivors of a Suicide Victim

■ "It was God's will."

■ "She's better off now."

■ "Why didn't you do something?"

■ "How did he do it?" Avoid curiosity and morbidity. The survivor may want to talk about the suicide, the events surrounding it, and the method of suicide, but if so, the survivor will initiate it.

Things That Might Be Said to the Survivor of a Suicide Victim

■ "I'm terribly sorry. I know there's no way I can imagine how awful this is for you."

■ "Is there anything you would like for me to do?"

■ "I'll be happy to stay with you if you want me to."

Ernest, the man who couldn't dance, could have claimed Macbeth's despairing lines as his own that somber Sunday afternoon he contemplated taking his life.

> Tomorrow, and tomorrow, and tomorrow,
> Creeps in this petty pace from day to day
> To the last syllable of recorded time,
> And all our yesterdays have lighted fools
> The way to dusty death. Out, out, brief candle!
> Life's but a walking shadow, a poor player
> That struts and frets his hour upon the stage
> And then is heard no more: it is a tale
> Told by an idiot, full of sound and fury,
> Signifying nothing.[3]

A disease of physical, psychological, social, and spiritual proportions had infected Ernest's life and led to an illness that can be fatal. He didn't know that the physiology of his brain had gone awry.

---

[3]William Shakespeare, *Macbeth,* Act 5, Scene 5.

He was unaware that his mind had lost the ability to correctly gauge his own emotions or to think clearly. He was unable to remain integrated in his culture of marriage, friends, and vocation. The light from his God no longer illuminated his path or warmed his spirit and he found neither solace nor strength in religion. He sank into the darkness of isolation, anger, and despair. Depression ripped out the heartstrings that thrummed with the dance of life. He couldn't hear the music of the future, let alone summon the strength to dance to it. The death certificate of persons with depression who commit suicide should list the cause of death as malignant sadness.

O God, you rule over your creation with tenderness,
Offering fresh hope in the midst of the most terrible misery.
We pray for our [beloved] whose soul is blackened by despair,
Infuse him with the pure light of your love.
As he curses the day he was born and yearns for oblivion,
Reveal to him the miracle of new birth
Which shall prepare him for the joys of heaven.[4]

Dimma, Seventh-Century Irish Monk

---

[4] *The HarperCollins Book of Prayers,* comp. Robert Van de Weyer (Edison, N.J.: Castle Books, 1997), 123–24.

A Cloud of Witnesses

Therefore, since we are surrounded by so great a cloud of witnesses,let us also lay aside every weight and the sin that clings so closely,and let us run with perseverance the race that is set before us.

HEBREWS 12:1

This is a list of artists, writers, journalists, poets, political leaders, actors, musicians, composers, and church laity who have suffered from some form of depression. The list is illustrative rather than comprehensive. The list was compiled from our own research, from those who have spoken publicly of their own depression, and the work of Kay Redfield Jamison in *Touched with Fire* (New York: Simon and Schuster, 1993).

Hans Christian Andersen
Irving Berlin
William Blake
Art Buchwald
John Bunyan
Winston Churchill
Pat Conroy
Charles Dickens
Emily Dickinson
Patty Duke
Edward Elgar
T. S. Eliot
Ralph Waldo Emerson
William Faulkner
Carrie Fisher
F. Scott Fitzgerald

Paul Gauguin
Graham Greene
Thomas Grey
George Frideric Handel
Ernest Hemingway
Gerard Manley Hopkins
Victor Hugo
John Keats
Abraham Lincoln
Robert Lowell
Martin Luther
Gustav Mahler
Herman Melville
Michelangelo
Edna St. Vincent Millay
Gregory of Nazianzus
Georgia O'Keefe
Jackson Pollock
Cole Porter
Sergey Rachmaninoff
Robert Schumann
John Starck
Rod Steiger
Robert Louis Stevenson
Dylan Thomas
Mark Twain
Vincent van Gogh
Tennessee Williams

Prayer for Those Unable to Dance

Holy God, how burdensome my past.
How heavy the days of my life.
How darkened tomorrow's dawn.
Shame breaks my heart.
Sorrow weights my waking hours.
Anger snares my soulless days.
Impotence haunts my every effort.
Loneliness stays my only companion.
Silence accompanies my prayers.
Sleeplessness steals away my night of rest.
And yet, and yet
I call your name, for you have written it on my heart.
I implore your healing, for you have dwelt among the sick.
I yearn for your deliverance, for you have faced the graveyard
    demon.
I crave your salvation, for you have raised your hand to bless.
I seek your light, for you have touched the darkness.
I desire life rather than death, for you have known and
    measured both.
I long for your music, for you have sung the world into being.
I long to dance again in the sweet feast of joy.
I ask not for quick and easy answers
But for deep and lasting peace.
I ask not for glory and power
But for grace and gentle strength.
I ask not for sumptuous banquets,
But for bread that feeds my soul.
I ask not for vintage wine,
But for the aperitif of kindly and kindred spirits.
I ask not for weedless gardens,
But for flowers to scent my arid life.
I ask not for prideful victory,
But for softened heart and generous love.
I ask not for parades and triumphal songs,
But for hope to hear the future's music.
I ask not for certitude and surety,

But for faith and courage to dance.
Let healing roll down like waters,
And your grace like an everlasting stream.
Let my soul dance in justice,
And my heart sing in kindness.
"May the God of hope fill me with all joy and peace in
  believing,
So that I may abound in hope by the power of the Holy Sprit."
Amen.

Victor L. Hunter